# THE Navarros' KITCHEN

A couple's guide to quick and
delicious healthy home cooking

# CONTENTS

## RECIPES

### CHEERS TO THAT

### START THE DAY RIGHT                      20

### POWER LUNCHES

### A TASTE OF OUR TRAVELS

### NAVARRO HOME COMFORTS

# OUR STORY

Since our weight loss journey started eight years ago, we've lost over six stone between us and maintained our goal weights for a few years now. Over this time, we've created delicious, healthy recipes to help support our weight loss goals, and we're so excited to finally be able to share these with you in this book.

When we started our weight loss journey, it was upsetting to see what was perceived as 'diet food'. We've always loved eating out (we still do) and trying foods from different countries, so we started looking at how we could make our favourite food in a healthier way. We started blogging and posting our recipes on Instagram as a little diary of what we were eating, but it very quickly became so much more than that. Seeing our recipes being enjoyed by thousands of people really spurred us on, and we've absolutely loved seeing how our content has helped others.

Healthy eating just doesn't have to be hard or boring! By cooking this way and creating hundreds of recipes over the years, it's become part of our everyday life, and it's always going to be. It doesn't have to take time, either: we've created recipes that fit in and around our working day. We both work full time, so we absolutely love recipes that are quick and easy to make, but we also love ones that make great family meals or can be eaten as leftovers. For us, it's about ease as well as taste. Our recipes include lunches that can be made in advance and taken as pack-ups, and so many of our main meals can be batch-cooked, pre-portioned and frozen. (But don't worry, we've also made sure to include some of our favourite weekend treats for when you have a little more time on your hands!)

Above all, we love to create recipes inspired by our heritage and travels. We think it's important to keep dishes as authentic as possible, so although we might use different ingredients and methods, we never compromise on taste. Some traditional recipes may be made using, for example, a tandoori oven or a rotisserie spit, but we create recipes in a way that achieves the same great taste and enjoyment but from the comfort of your home kitchen.

We hope you love recreating our recipes as much as we loved creating them! Don't forget to tag us in your pictures when you cook one of our recipes @TopChefNavarros_SW! We'd love to see them.

*Zoe & Clinton*

# OUR STORE CUPBOARD
# AND FREEZER STAPLES

## DRIED HERBS AND SPICES

This one's the most important of all the cooking staples: our herb and spice racks are a very prominent part of our kitchen. Most of our recipes were originally created by playing with herbs and spices; just adding a little here and there until we got the flavour right. Many popular flavours, like Cajun or peri-peri, have ready-made spice mixes, and while these are fab, be careful as they can have added sugar and oils.

## FRESH HERBS AND AROMATICS

We always have fresh lemons and limes in the fridge as this is our preference when cooking, but we also have easy-access bottles of concentrate too. Typically, the juice of 1 lemon or lime is equivalent to 2 tbsp of concentrate. Fresh chillies, ginger and garlic are also brilliant for adding flavour, and you'll see these used in so many of our recipes. The frozen and jarred equivalents of these make great speedy alternatives. We also love to use potted fresh herbs. They're so flavoursome and you can buy them from most supermarkets. These will last a long time on your kitchen windowsill or, better still, you can plant them and start a little herb patch in your garden.

## VINEGARS AND CONDIMENTS

There are many different vinegars and condiments out there, but a few of our favourites are: balsamic vinegar, red and white wine vinegar, apple cider vinegar, Worcestershire sauce or Henderson's Relish, soy sauce, and honey. When making dishes from around the world, these are key for adding depth of flavour and bringing the recipe together.

Note: If you're making a vegetarian-friendly version of a dish, swap Worcestershire sauce for Henderson's Relish (as it doesn't contain anchovies).

## FROZEN AND TINNED VEGETABLES

Chopped tomatoes and passata are our most frequently used tinned ingredients. They make the base of many of our sauces and they're a great, healthy alternative to cream-based dishes. In our recipes, we mostly use fresh vegetables, but there are so many options now for frozen, tinned, and pre-prepared vegetables. For speed and ease, you can easily make swaps to these instead.

## COOKING SPRAYS

Most of our recipes will use cooking spray when frying or baking. There are two different types: one is an oil, such as olive, sunflower or rapeseed oil, which is usually 2 calories per spray, and this the preference in our recipes. The other version is more of a creamy oil spray which comes in several varieties and is usually 1 calorie per spray.

## BREAD

We use a variety of bread throughout the book. We often choose gluten-free or wholemeal varieties as they tend to have more fibre, but we also love a brioche bun with a burger and Greek-style pitta breads. Of course, you can swap out your preferred bread in any of our recipes. Since bread doesn't tend to have the longest shelf life, we always keep a stash of our favourites in the freezer and just defrost them as and when we need them.

## CHEESE AND DAIRY

Cheese and yoghurt are a great way of getting calcium into meals. Most of them come in a reduced fat variety, so you can make healthy meals without having to compromise on taste. We always make sure we have 0% fat authentic Greek yoghurt in the fridge, as well as a variety of cheeses such as cheddar, mozzarella, halloumi and feta.

## RICE, PASTA AND PULSES

These are already staples in most households! They're great for making quick and easy dishes, and with so many flavour combinations, the possibilities are endless. Note: If you prefer, you can swap out the dried variety with the microwaveable pouches or frozen bags.

# OUR TOP KITCHEN GADGETS

We wanted to share some staple tools and gadgets that help us in the kitchen. These aren't 100% essential, but they're great for making cooking quicker and easier!

## SLOW COOKER

This is one of the ultimate kitchen appliances, especially if you have a busy working lifestyle. Just pop the ingredients in and leave it to work its magic. Nothing beats the feeling of coming home to the beautiful smell of a meal that's cooked and ready for you. These are super versatile and can cook anything from curries and stews to joints of meat and desserts. They're also great for batch cooking and when cooking for lots of people.

## AIR FRYER

Air fryers have become super popular, and they come in all different types, shapes, and sizes. We absolutely love ours and use it so much more than we do our oven. Air fryers allow you to save time and cook meals quicker, but they can also be more affordable than traditional ovens. We love to use the paddle air fryer for our fries as it keeps them constantly moving and makes the best evenly crispy chips. For other recipes, we recommend the basket or drawer-style air fryers. Each of our recipes states a preferred cooking method, and this may be the oven or air fryer, but this can easily be adjusted depending on what you prefer to use. The table below can help with some approximate temperature conversions:

| GAS | STATIC OVEN | FAN OVEN | AIR FRYER |
|-----|-------------|----------|-----------|
| 1 | 140 | 120 | 110 |
| 2 | 150 | 130 | 120 |
| 3 | 170 | 150 | 140 |
| 4 | 180 | 160 | 150 |
| 5 | 190 | 170 | 160 |
| 6 | 200 | 180 | 170 |
| 7 | 220 | 200 | 190 |
| 8 | 240 | 220 | 210 |

When cooking in an air fryer, you should also cook for around 20% less time than in a traditional oven. Ovens and air fryers can vary, so be sure to check and alter times and temperatures according to your model. Air fryer cooking temperatures can be anywhere between 10-20°c below the required temperature for a fan oven.

### BLENDER OR FOOD PROCESSOR

These are an absolute must in the kitchen for us. They take the hard work out of so many kitchen jobs, such as making breadcrumbs, blitzing sauces, and chopping veg. There are so many available on the market: hand blenders, mini choppers, food processors, smoothie blenders, and more. By just having one of these, you can save so much time when prepping your weekly meals.

### CHIP CUTTER

We love our chip cutter. It's a real time saver and makes perfectly shaped fries. We enjoy ours with the skin on; all you have to do is put the potato in, push the handle down, and the fries pop out. You'll find these in most online retailers.

### TEMPERATURE PROBE

A temperature meat probe is a brilliant kitchen gadget. It's handy for larger pieces of meat or chicken dishes and helps ensure that the meat is cooked to the right temperature. It also makes sure you avoid overcooking, because it'll help you remove the meat from the oven at the right time. They're great for barbecues too, since the temperature can vary a lot on the grill.

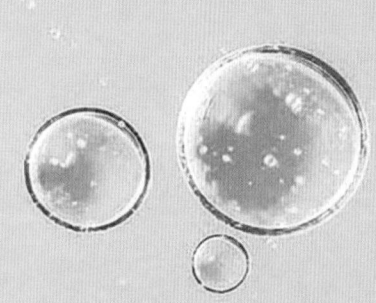

# CHEERS
# TO THAT

# ALCOHOL-FREE MULLED WINE

Prep time: 5 minutes | Cooking time: 15 minutes | Serves: 6 plus | Gluten-Free, Vegetarian, Dairy-Free | Calories: 6

We love a mulled wine during the festive period, but they can usually be full of sugar and, of course, alcohol. This alcohol and sugar-free version still has all the flavour of mulled wine and can be enjoyed any time.

## INGREDIENTS

600ml sugar-free cherry and berry squash (we use Winter Spice Squash)

2.5L water

2 mulled wine bags

2 cinnamon sticks

2 oranges, cut into quarters

## METHOD

Add all ingredients to a large saucepan and place onto the hob on a high heat.

Bring to the boil, then turn down to a simmer and leave to cook for 10 minutes.

Serve directly from the pan in heatproof glasses.

## NOTES

This recipe is great for parties. Make the recipe in a slow cooker and keep on low for the whole evening – it will also make your house smell beautiful too!

# COKE
# FLOAT

Prep time: 5 minutes | Serves: 1 | Gluten-Free, Vegetarian | Calories: 55

This one is an iconic American treat but it's also one my dad used to make for me and my siblings when we were kids. This one's made with only two ingredients, but it can also be topped with a squirty whipped cream!

## INGREDIENTS

1 scoop low calorie vanilla ice cream (approx. 60g)

1 can diet cola drink

## METHOD

Scoop the ice cream into a tall glass.

Pour the cola over the top, making sure to leave about an inch from top of the glass (as the ice cream froth will expand and rise).

Serve immediately and enjoy (you may need a spoon, too!).

## NOTES

Swap the cola for lemonade or any flavoured fizzy drink of your choice.

# STRAWBERRY
# LEMONADE

Prep time: 10 minutes | Serves: 2 | Vegetarian, Gluten-Free, Dairy-Free | Calories: 56

A lovely and refreshing summer drink that combines zingy lemonade with fresh strawberries. This drink is perfect for those summer barbecues and is best prepared the night before.

## INGREDIENTS

200g strawberries

100ml sugar-free lemonade (still or slightly flat works better)

100ml water

1 tbsp honey

3 lemons, juiced

## METHOD

Top and halve the strawberries and add to a blender with the other ingredients.

Blitz until smooth, then pour through a sieve to remove any of the strawberry seeds. Serve over ice cubes.

## NOTES

This is best made the night before and left chilled in the fridge to enjoy the next day.

# GREEK-STYLE FRAPPÉ

Prep time: 5 minutes | Serves: 1 | Vegetarian, Gluten-Free, Dairy-Free* | Calories: 18

Frappé is a very popular coffee drink in Greece - it's on every drinks menu and it's one of our favourites. It's usually made with a few teaspoons of sugar, so we made this low-sugar version that tastes just as good!

## INGREDIENTS

2 tsp coffee granules

2 tsp granulated sweetener

50ml water

3-4 ice cubes

Cold water

Dash of milk (dairy or non-dairy*)

## METHOD

Whisk together the coffee, sweetener, and 50ml water. This should expand and create a whipped foam.
Add the ice cubes to a tall glass, then pour in the whipped coffee.
Fill the glass with cold water, then finish with a dash of milk.

## NOTES

Serve with a side of ice-cold water so you can top up the glass for a longer drink.

# HAZELNUT OAT COFFEE SLUSHIE

Prep time: 5 minutes | Serves: 1 | Dairy-Free, Vegetarian, Gluten-Free | Calories: 70

If you are coffee lovers like us, then you must try this one! It's a super refreshing drink that's beautiful in the summer, and all you need is a few ingredients and a blender! This one is dairy-free, but you could use any milk and swap out the syrup for other flavours, too.

## INGREDIENTS

1 espresso shot, cooled

150ml oat milk, chilled

1 tsp sugar-free hazelnut syrup

8 ice cubes

## METHOD

Add all the ingredients to a blender or smoothie maker and pulse until fully blended.
Serve immediately in a tall glass with a straw, and top with squirty cream for that extra bit of indulgence.

## NOTES

If you can't make espresso at home, use a teaspoon of instant coffee mixed with 40ml boiling water.

# VIRGIN MOJITO

Prep time: 5 minutes | Serves: 1 | Vegetarian, Gluten-Free, Dairy-Free | Calories: 6

A fresh and light cocktail with sweet, subtle hints of lime and mint. This can easily be made as an individual drink or as a pitcher, so it's perfect for a summer drink in the garden or at parties.

## INGREDIENTS

1 lime, cut into quarters, plus extra for garnish

2 tsp granulated sweetener

6 fresh mint leaves

Crushed ice

Soda water

## METHOD

Place the lime and sweetener into a tall glass.

Crush the lime and muddle, using either a muddler or small rolling pin, for about 30 seconds to release the juices.

Smash the mint leaves in your hands to release their aroma, then place these into the glass. Muddle with the lime and sweetener.

Add a handful of crushed ice to the glass and fill to the top with the soda water.

Garnish with a slice of lime and more mint leaves to serve.

## NOTES

Use sugar-free lemonade instead of soda water if you like it a little sweeter. You can also add 30ml white rum to the same recipe if you want to enjoy the alcoholic version.

# START THE DAY RIGHT

# BERRY BIRCHER MUESLI

Prep time: 10 minutes, plus overnight refrigeration | Serves: 1 | Vegetarian, Gluten-Free | Calories: 335

A beautiful breakfast that can be prepared the night before. This recipe is a bit like overnight oats, but by soaking the oats first and mashing them with fruit, the oats take on loads of delicious flavour.

## INGREDIENTS

40g porridge oats

120ml boiling water

1 banana

1 tsp granulated sweetener

120g frozen berries

100g fat-free natural yoghurt

1 tsp vanilla essence

## METHOD

Add the oats to a bowl, pour over 120ml boiling water and mix well. Add the banana, sweetener, and berries, and mash it all together. Cover the bowl and leave in the fridge overnight.

When ready, mix the yoghurt with the vanilla essence and layer in a glass or Mason jar with the berry oats.

## NOTES

Try a flavoured yoghurt or different kinds of fruit to experiment with flavour combinations.

# TOFFEE APPLE OVERNIGHT OATS

Prep time: 10 minutes, plus overnight refrigeration | Serves: 1 | Vegetarian, Gluten-Free | Calories: 345

A super quick and filling breakfast that can be made the night before. Simply pop it in the fridge overnight, give it a quick stir in the morning, and it's ready to eat. This one's a versatile recipe that can be adapted using any fruit or yoghurt.

## INGREDIENTS

40g porridge oats

1 sweet apple, grated (Pink Lady apples work well)

200g fat-free toffee yoghurt

1 tbsp toffee sauce

Pinch of cinnamon (optional)

## METHOD

Add half of the oats to a lidded jar or glass and top with half of the grated apple.

Spoon in half of the yoghurt, then layer with the rest of the oats and the remaining apple.

Top with the last of the yoghurt, drizzle over the toffee sauce, and sprinkle with cinnamon.

Pop in the fridge overnight and, when ready, give a quick stir before enjoying.

## NOTES

Swap the apple for sliced bananas to make a yummy banoffee version.

# WATERMELON PIZZA

Prep time: 10 minutes | Serves: 1 | Vegetarian, Gluten-Free | Calories: 205

A breakfast or dessert with all the summer vibes. This is a fun way of serving a fruit salad and it's one that children will love getting involved in, too!

## INGREDIENTS

1 watermelon

2 tbsp 0% fat Greek yoghurt

3 strawberries, sliced

6 raspberries

8-10 blueberries

1 tbsp runny honey

## METHOD

Using a large, sharp knife, cut a slice from the centre of the watermelon (approximately 1 inch thick).

Remove any of the visible seeds, if desired, then spread the yoghurt over the watermelon slice.

Scatter the fresh fruit over the top and drizzle with honey.

## NOTES

We've used some of our favourite toppings in this recipe, but you can use any yoghurt, fruit, seeds, nuts, or toppings of your choosing.

# BREAKFAST BAGEL BURGER

Prep time: 10 minutes | Cooking time: 20 minutes | Serves: 2 | Calories: 570

The ultimate breakfast burger! Juicy, filling and full of flavour. This is a go-to for us on a weekend and keeps us full for the day.

## INGREDIENTS

2 hash browns

1 onion, finely chopped

1 tbsp granulated sweetener

6 reduced fat pork sausages, skin removed

4 rashers of bacon, fat removed

70g halloumi

2 bagels (we use thin seeded bagels)

Leaf salad

2 tbsp apple sauce

## METHOD

Cook the hash browns as per the packet instructions.

Meanwhile, heat some cooking oil spray in a frying pan and sauté the onion until soft and golden-brown in colour. Add the sweetener and cook for 30 seconds, stirring continuously.

Remove the onions from heat and set aside. Then, once cooled, add the onions to a bowl with the sausage meat and mix.

Split the mixture into 4 equal portions and mould into patties. Cook in a frying pan on a medium-high heat for 6-7 minutes on each side or until cooked through. Fry the bacon in the same pan.

When the patties and bacon are cooked, move them to the side of the pan, turn the heat down to medium, and fry the halloumi.

Once cooked through, build your bagel by stacking the ingredients as follows: bagel base, leaf salad, patty, bacon, halloumi, patty, apple sauce, hash brown, then the bagel top. Pierce with a skewer to hold the ingredients in place and enjoy.

# CHEESY CHORIZO SCRAMBLED EGG

Prep time: 5 minutes | Cooking time: 10 minutes | Serves: 2 | Calories: 547

This recipe is a lovely quick and easy one, perfect for breakfasts. We love adding different ingredients to the scrambled egg, especially chorizo, as it releases so much flavour when cooking.

## INGREDIENTS

1 tsp olive oil

1 onion, chopped

50g chorizo, chopped

5 eggs

50ml semi-skimmed milk

2 wholemeal breakfast muffins

50g cheddar cheese, grated

1 tsp paprika

Pinch of salt and pepper

## METHOD

In a large frying pan, heat the oil and then add the chopped onion and chorizo. Fry for 5 minutes until the onion begins to soften and the oils are released from the chorizo.

Meanwhile, whisk the eggs and milk together in a bowl or jug. Pour them into the pan and leave for 10 seconds, then slowly start to mix and break the egg up as it starts to set.

Keep stirring until the egg scrambles but be careful not to fully cook them. Slice your muffins in half and pop them in the toaster at this point.

Turn off the heat and add the cheese and paprika to the eggs, seasoning with salt and pepper to taste. Stir for a further 1-2 minutes, until they are fully cooked and cheese has melted.

Serve your cheesy chorizo scrambled eggs on top of the toasted muffins.

## NOTES
Feel free to swap the muffins for any bread of your choice or perhaps even potato waffles.

# CORFIOT
# BREAKFAST

Prep time: 10 minutes | Cooking time: 30 minutes | Serves: 2 | Calories: 498

This is a breakfast we fell in love with a few years ago in Corfu. It's like an English cooked breakfast but it has a sweet, spiced tomato sauce and poached eggs.

## INGREDIENTS

1 x 400g tin of chopped tomatoes

½ tsp cayenne pepper

1 tsp cinnamon

1 tsp oregano

1 tsp fine sea salt

1 tsp ground black pepper

2 tbsp red wine vinegar

1 large orange

4 lean bacon medallions

4 low fat pork sausages

1 tbsp white wine vinegar

4 eggs

2 slices wholemeal bread

90g feta cheese

Fresh dill, or 1 tsp dried dill tips

## METHOD

Heat the tinned tomatoes in a large pan and add the cayenne pepper, cinnamon, oregano, salt, pepper and red wine vinegar. Bring to a boil, then turn down to a simmer and cover. Check and stir every 5 minutes, adding a touch of water if required so the sauce doesn't dry out.

Grill the sausages and bacon or pop in the air fryer until cooked through.

Meanwhile, heat a separate pan of water, add the white wine vinegar and bring to a boil. While the pan of water is heating up, peel the orange, break into segments and set aside.

When the water is boiling, turn down to a simmer and stir with a whisk to create a whirlpool. Crack one egg in carefully and poach for 3 minutes before removing and placing in a bowl with some kitchen towel. Repeat with the remaining 3 eggs.

Toast the bread to a nice golden colour and cut each slice in half.

Place two poached eggs in the centre of each plate, cover with tomato sauce, and top with a sprinkling of crumbled feta.

Place the bacon and sausages around the outside of the plate along with the orange segments and toast.

Sprinkle the dill over the top and enjoy.

# SHAKSHUKA

Prep time: 10 minutes | Cooking time: 30 minutes | Serves: 2 | Vegetarian, Gluten-Free, Dairy-Free | Calories: 204

Shakshuka is a popular dish around the world, and it's one we love too. A naturally healthy option for breakfast or brunch, this recipe is packed full of vegetables and is super easy to make in just one pan.

## INGREDIENTS

Cooking oil spray

1 red onion, sliced

2 red or yellow peppers, sliced

2 cloves of garlic, crushed

1 tsp fine sea salt

1½ tsp cumin

1 tsp paprika

2 tsp mild chilli powder

2 x 400g tins of chopped tomatoes

4 eggs

Pinch of fresh parsley leaves, to serve

## METHOD

Place a skillet or deep frying pan on a medium heat and spray with cooking oil spray.

Add the onion, peppers and garlic and fry for 5 minutes until softened.

Stir in the salt and dried spices and cook for a further 2-3 minutes.

Add the tinned tomatoes, stir, and bring to the boil. Then, turn down to a simmer and cook for 15 minutes.

Using a spatula or spoon, make four holes in the sauce and crack an egg into each one.

If using an ovenproof pan or skillet, place into a preheated oven at 200°c/180°c fan for 5 minutes to bake. If using a frying pan, cover with a lid and continue to cook on a low heat for 4-5 minutes.

Sprinkle fresh parsley over the top and serve.

## NOTES

Serve with garlic yoghurt and our Easy Flatbreads (see page 172) to mop up the sauce.

# POWER
# LUNCHES

# BUTTERNUT SQUASH AND RED PEPPER SOUP

Prep time: 10 minutes | Cooking time: 30 minutes | Serves: 4 | Vegetarian, Dairy-Free | Calories: 98

Soups are great for making in batches. We love to make this one and take it to work for lunch in the winter (but it's still soup-er nice to have all year round). This is an easy recipe that only uses a few ingredients, and it's even easier if you have a soup maker.

## INGREDIENTS

Cooking oil spray

2 red peppers, chopped

1 onion, chopped

1 clove of garlic, chopped

1 medium butternut squash, deseeded, peeled, and chopped

800ml vegetable stock

½ tsp thyme

1 tbsp fat-free natural yoghurt, to serve

## METHOD

Spray a large pan with cooking oil and fry the red pepper, onion and garlic for around 5 minutes until softened.

Add the butternut squash to the pan with the vegetable stock. Bring to the boil, then turn down to a simmer and leave for 20 minutes or until the butternut squash has fully softened.

Remove from the heat, add the thyme and season to taste with salt and pepper.

Blend using a hand blender, or transfer to a food processor and blitz until smooth.

Serve with a spoonful of natural yoghurt on top, if desired.

## NOTES

For ease, you can use pre-chopped, packaged butternut squash.

# CAPRESE
# PANINI

Prep time: 5 minutes | Cooking time: 5 minutes | Serves: 2 | Gluten-Free, Vegetarian | Calories: 258

All the caprese salad vibes in a lovely crispy panini! Filled with fresh tomatoes, mozzarella, and pesto, this makes a delicious lunch in under 10 minutes.

## INGREDIENTS

2 gluten-free ciabattas (or your bread of choice)

4 level tbsp reduced fat pesto

1 large vine tomato, sliced

100g mozzarella

Cooking oil spray

## METHOD

Slice the ciabattas in half lengthways and spray the outsides with cooking oil spray.

Spread 1 tablespoon of pesto on the inside of each ciabatta half.

Layer half the mozzarella and tomato in each sandwich, then pop into a panini press or similar press-style grill.

Leave to toast for 4-5 minutes or until the mozzarella has melted and the outside is crispy and golden.

Serve with a leafy salad and balsamic vinegar glaze.

## NOTES

For this recipe, we've used a press-style grill, but this can also be toasted in a pan for 5 minutes on each side, using a spatula to press the panini down.

# PIZZA POTATO
# WAFFLES

Prep time: 5 minutes | Cooking time: 10 minutes | Serves: 1 | Calories: 350

Did you know the quickest way to cook a potato waffle is in a toaster?! These are a staple in our house, and we always keep them in the freezer for super quick dinners like this one.

## INGREDIENTS

2 potato waffles

2 tbsp tomato purée

40g grated mozzarella

Toppings of your choice (such as pepperoni, chicken, peppers, red onion and sweetcorn)

## METHOD

Cook the potato waffles as per the packet instructions. (For the fastest method, pop in the toaster for about 5 minutes.)

Pop onto a plate and spread with the tomato purée before adding the desired toppings and finishing with the grated mozzarella.

Pop under the grill or in the oven at 200°c/180°c fan for 5 minutes to heat through and melt the cheese. You can also cook this one in the airfryer.

## NOTES

These would be just as amazing using crispy hash browns!

# PERI-PERI CHICKEN AND SPICY RICE

Prep time: 10 minutes | Cooking time: 25 minutes | Serves: 2 | Gluten-Free, Dairy-Free | Calories: 525

Our spicy rice is inspired by a famous restaurant and we batch-cook it often as it's great for taking to work. We pair it with peri-peri spiced chicken to make it into a full delicious meal.

## INGREDIENTS

### For the peri-peri chicken

2 chicken breasts

3 tbsp passata

1 tbsp lemon juice

1 tsp paprika

½ tsp cumin

1 tsp parsley

½ tsp cayenne pepper

1 tsp dried chilli flakes

1 tsp ground sea salt

½ tsp turmeric

1 tbsp Worcestershire sauce or Henderson's Relish

### For the spicy rice

150g long grain rice

1 chicken stock cube

1 yellow pepper, chopped

1 red pepper, chopped

1 red onion, chopped

Handful of frozen peas

1 tsp paprika

1 tsp cumin

1 tsp turmeric

1 tsp chilli powder

## METHOD

If using an oven, preheat to 200°c/180°c fan.

Combine the chicken with the passata, lemon juice, dried spices, and Worcestershire sauce.

Wrap the chicken in foil and cook for 20 minutes in the oven or air fryer. Then, unwrap the chicken and cook for a further 5 minutes uncovered.

While the chicken is cooking, cook the rice as per the packet instructions, adding the chicken stock cube to the cooking water.

Meanwhile, spray a large frying pan with cooking oil and fry the peppers and onions. Cook for 8-10 minutes, then stir in the peas and spices and cook for a further 2-3 minutes. Turn off the heat and leave in the pan.

Remove the cooked chicken from the oven, wrap it back up in the foil and leave to rest.

When the rice is cooked, add it to the frying pan with the onions, peppers, peas and spices and gently stir through until the rice takes on the colour of the spices. Turn the heat to low to warm through, if required.

Slice the chicken breasts and serve on top of the spicy rice.

## NOTES

We love to coat the chicken in our own peri-peri mix, but if you prefer, there are lots of store-bought sauces that could be used instead.

# BALSAMIC ROAST VEG WITH GIANT COUSCOUS

Prep time: 10 minutes | Cooking time: 25 minutes | Serves: 4 | Vegetarian, Dairy-Free | Calories: 110

We love couscous but there is just something special about the giant kind. It has a lovely texture and takes on flavours so well! We often make couscous dishes as a side for meals, but it's a good one to make in batches to take to work as it can be eaten hot or cold. You could even add chicken to this for extra protein.

## INGREDIENTS

1 red pepper, chopped

1 yellow pepper, chopped

1 courgette, chopped

1 red onion, chopped

Balsamic vinegar

Cooking oil spray

150g giant couscous

1 tsp paprika

1 tsp oregano

## METHOD

Preheat the oven to 210°c/190°c fan.

Add the chopped pepper, courgette and onion into a bowl with a good splash of balsamic vinegar and mix well.

Spray a baking tray with cooking oil spray, transfer all the balsamic and veg onto the tray, then spray again with the cooking oil.

Pop in the oven and roast for about 25 minutes or until softened and slightly charred.

Meanwhile, cook the giant couscous as per the packet instructions, then drain and transfer to a large bowl.

Once the vegetables have cooked, add to the couscous with the paprika, oregano, and a couple more splashes of balsamic vinegar.

Stir through, serve, and enjoy.

## NOTES

Most supermarkets sell giant couscous, but if you can't find it, this recipe works just as well with normal couscous.

# TUNA CRUNCH
# PASTA

Prep time: 10 minutes | Cooking time: 10 minutes | Serves: 3-4 | Calories: 448

We often make batches of this for a packed lunch to take to work, as you can make the portion sizes as small or as large as you like. It's also great for buffets, or as a side dish for summer barbecues.

## INGREDIENTS

380g pasta (fusilli works well)

1 red pepper

1 red onion

7-8cm cucumber

2 spring onions

2 tins of tuna chunks

3 tbsp 0% fat Greek yoghurt

2 tbsp light mayonnaise

1 tbsp lemon juice

1 tsp English mustard

## METHOD

Cook the pasta in a pan of boiling salted water, then drain and cool by rinsing it under cold water in a colander. Pop the pasta to one side for now.

While the pasta is cooking, chop the red pepper, red onion and cucumber into bite-size chunks and thinly slice the spring onion. Combine the prepared vegetables in a large bowl.

Drain the tuna and add it to the bowl of vegetables. Mix well until combined.

In a separate bowl, mix the Greek yoghurt, mayonnaise, lemon juice, and mustard until well combined.

Add the pasta to the vegetables and tuna, then stir in the dressing. Mix well so everything is evenly distributed before serving chilled or at room temperature.

## NOTES

Our preference for this recipe is to use tuna chunks in brine, but any tinned tuna can be used here.

# PRAWN COCKTAIL

Prep time: 10 minutes | Serves: 4 | Gluten-Free | Calories: 104

An absolute classic of a dish and a very popular choice as a starter. This recipe is a healthier version of the traditional Thousand Island sauce, but it still has all the lovely flavour and colour.

## INGREDIENTS

130g 0% fat Greek yoghurt

2 tbsp lemon juice

2 tbsp tomato purée

1 tsp paprika

½ tsp dried parsley

1 tbsp white wine vinegar

1 tbsp Worcestershire sauce

400g king prawns, cooked and peeled

1 lettuce leaf

Fresh chives, chopped

1 lemon, cut into wedges, to serve

## METHOD

Mix the Greek yoghurt, lemon juice and tomato purée together in a bowl. Stir in the paprika, parsley, white wine vinegar and Worcestershire sauce, then season to taste and add the king prawns.

Layer in a glass or bowl on top of a lettuce leaf and finish with a sprinkling of fresh chives and paprika. Serve with lemon wedges.

# PESTO ORZO WITH CHICKEN AND FETA

Prep time: 5 minutes | Cooking time: 10 minutes | Serves: 4 | Calories: 184

This is an easy dish to make for lunches at home, but another one that's great to make in batches to take to work. It's a super versatile recipe that you can fill with any salad vegetables you might have in.

## INGREDIENTS

200g orzo

150g cherry tomatoes, halved

200g cooked chicken, cut into chunks

1 green pepper, chopped

3 spring onions, sliced

4 tbsp reduced fat pesto

80g feta

## METHOD

Cook the orzo as per the packet instructions, then drain and rinse with cold water.

Add the orzo to a large bowl with the cherry tomatoes, cooked chicken, pepper, and spring onion. Then, spoon in the pesto and stir well to combine.

Crumble in the feta and give it a final, light mix.

Serve and enjoy.

# A TASTE OF
# OUR TRAVELS

# BEEF
# KOFTES

Prep time: 10 minutes, plus 30 minutes refrigeration | Cooking time: 15 minutes | Serves: 6 | Dairy-Free, Gluten-Free | Calories: 145

We love this dish in the summer, and it's one we quite often make when we're having a barbecue. These are amazing flame-grilled on the barbecue, but they can also be pan fried, grilled, or cooked in the oven.

## INGREDIENTS

500g 5% fat beef steak mince

1 jarred roasted red pepper, finely chopped

1 egg

1 tsp ground nutmeg

1 tsp paprika

1 tsp fresh parsley, chopped

1 tsp fresh coriander, chopped

1 tsp cumin

1 tsp chilli flakes

1 clove of garlic, crushed and chopped

1 tbsp Worcestershire sauce or Henderson's Relish

1 tsp fine sea salt

Cooking oil spray

## METHOD

Preheat the grill or barbecue. If using an oven, preheat to 200°c/180°c fan.

Mix all the ingredients, except the cooking oil, in a large bowl and knead for 3-4 minutes.

Split the mixture into 6 equal portions and roll into sausage shapes. Then, place the koftes into the fridge for a minimum of 30 minutes to firm up.

When ready to cook, remove the koftes from the fridge and prepare a bowl of cold water. Press a skewer down into the centre of each kofte, then turn it gradually to flatten the kofte and wrap it around the skewer. Wet your hands to help shape it.

Spray the kofte with cooking oil spray and cook under a grill or over hot coals for 10 minutes until cooked. Turn the koftes every couple of minutes to keep them even in colour and to stop them sticking to the grill. If using an oven, cook for 20 minutes and turn halfway through.

## NOTES

We love to have these with our Easy Flatbreads (see page 172), tzatziki (see page 134) and a fresh salad.

# BUTTER CHICKEN (MURGH MAKHANI)

Prep time: 10 minutes, plus 2 hours marinating | Cooking time: 45 minutes | Serves: 3-4 | Gluten-Free (contains nuts) | Calories: 330

Zoe lived on butter chicken when we visited Northern India for a sponsored trek in the Himalayas. It's a very popular Indian dish, so we absolutely had to make it at home. It always brings back good memories.

## INGREDIENTS

**For the curry**

500g chicken breast, diced

25g butter

3 cloves of garlic, crushed and chopped

1 onion, diced

3 tbsp tomato purée

1 tsp ginger paste

1 tsp garam masala

2 tsp granulated sweetener

350ml chicken stock

10g almond flakes, to garnish (optional)

**For the chicken marinade**

200g fat-free natural yoghurt

2 tbsp lemon juice

2 tsp tandoori curry powder

2 tsp ground cumin

2 tsp paprika

2 tsp mild chilli powder

## METHOD

Combine the marinade ingredients in a bowl with the chicken and stir to coat. Leave to marinate in the fridge for at least 2 hours (overnight is best).

Melt the butter in a large frying pan over a medium heat, add the garlic and onion, and fry for 5-6 minutes until softened.

Add the tomato purée, ginger, garam masala and sweetener and stir through. Cook for 2-3 minutes before adding the chicken stock and bringing to the boil.

Add the marinated chicken and turn down to a simmer. Leave on a low heat and cook for 30 minutes uncovered.

In a separate pan, toast the almond flakes for 3-4 minutes until they turn golden, then set them aside.

Top the butter chicken with the toasted almond flakes and serve.

## NOTES

This one's great with our Saag Rice (see page 182).

# CREAMY PEA AND PANCETTA GNOCCHI

Prep time: 10 minutes | Cooking time: 15 minutes | Serves: 2 | Calories: 600

A super quick, easy and filling recipe that's perfect for those midweek meals. It only uses a handful of ingredients, but it's packed with flavour.

## INGREDIENTS

400g gnocchi

75g pancetta, cut into cubes

2 cloves of garlic, finely chopped

100ml chicken stock

100g reduced fat cream cheese

100g frozen peas

30g parmesan, finely grated

## METHOD

Cook the gnocchi as per the packet instructions.

Meanwhile, heat a large frying pan with a few spritzes of cooking spray oil and add the pancetta. Cook until crispy, then add the garlic and fry for a further 2 minutes.

Add the chicken stock, cream cheese, and peas, then stir through and cook for 2-3 minutes.

Drain the gnocchi and add this to the pan along with the parmesan cheese. Stir to combine.

Serve and enjoy.

## NOTES

You can swap the gnocchi for any type of pasta; just cook as per the packet instructions and combine with the sauce.

# CHICKEN GYROS

Prep time: 20 minutes | Cooking time: 40 minutes | Serves: 2 | Calories: 635

There was no way this recipe wasn't going to be in our book - it's our absolute favourite and one we know so many of you will love too! We visit Corfu every year, it's like our second home, and we love having these while we're out there, but we also love making a healthier, homemade version. These are traditionally cooked on a rotating spit, which is where the word 'gyros' comes from, but they can easily be cooked in the oven, air fryer, or pan too.

## INGREDIENTS

5-6 skinless chicken thighs, fat removed

1 lemon, juiced

1 clove of garlic, crushed and chopped

1 tsp oregano

1 tsp thyme

1 tsp rosemary

½ tsp paprika

½ tsp ground clove

1 tsp fine sea salt

½ tsp ground black pepper

Cooking oil spray

Our Fantastic Fries (see page 184)

Wraps or Easy Flatbreads (see page 172)

Tzatziki (see page 134)

1 red onion, sliced

1 large tomato, sliced

Chip spice

## METHOD

Preheat the oven to 210°c/190°c fan.

Add the chicken thighs to a bowl with the lemon, garlic, oregano, thyme, rosemary, paprika, ground clove, salt and pepper. Mix well to coat the chicken.

Place the thighs side by side in a deep ovenproof dish or loaf tin and press down tightly, then cook in the oven for 20 minutes. While the chicken is cooking, prepare the chips or fries.

After 20 minutes, drain some of the juices from the chicken and cook for a further 20 minutes.

When the thighs are fully cooked, remove them from the oven, cover with foil, and leave to rest for 5 minutes.

Meanwhile, warm the flatbreads in a large pan. When warmed through, turn off the heat but leave them in the pan to keep warm.

Remove the chicken from the tin and slice it into chunks.

To make the gyros, place the flatbread in the corner of a sheet of greaseproof paper, approx. 14"x 10" in size.

Spread some tzatziki down the centre of the flatbread, followed by some onion, sliced tomato, chopped chicken, and a handful of chips.

Take the corners of the paper either side of the flatbread and wrap them around the gyro, then twist the remaining paper at the bottom tightly and fold it back to secure the filling. It can also be served open, if preferred.

Sprinkle chip spice over the top and enjoy.

## NOTES

We love this method as it keeps the chicken thighs lovely and juicy, but for a faster method, cook them in a pan or air fryer.

# GREEK FETA-STUFFED BIFTEKI

Prep time: 5 minutes, plus 10 minutes refrigeration | Cooking time: 20 minutes | Serves: 2 | Calories: 468

Bifteki is like the Greek version of a burger, and this one is filled with delicious feta. Packed with flavour and super simple to make, these are usually served with potatoes and make a really hearty meal.

## INGREDIENTS

Cooking oil spray

1 red onion, finely diced

500g 5% fat beef steak mince

1 egg

2 tsp fresh mint leaves, chopped or 2 tsp dried mint

2 tsp oregano

1 tsp thyme

1 tsp fine sea salt

1 tsp ground black pepper

80g feta cheese, cut into 4 equal blocks

## METHOD

Heat a frying pan with cooking oil spray and sauté the onion until softened. Remove from the heat and allow to cool.

Add the minced beef, egg, cooled onion, mint, oregano, thyme, salt, and pepper to a large bowl and mix well using your hands. Give the mixture a good kneading to get all the flavours into the meat, then pop into the fridge for 10 minutes.

Split the mixture into 4 equal patties, then flatten to a round shape in your hand. Place a cube of feta into the centre of each patty and wrap the mince around it to ensure the feta is covered and sealed.

Grill for 6-8 minutes on each side or, for an even better taste, cook on a barbecue over hot coals.

# ITALIAN
# PANUOZZO

Prep time: 5 minutes | Cooking time: 5 minutes | Serves: 2 | Calories: 400

These are delicious Italian pizza-style sandwiches that originate from the Campania region. We first tried them on a trip to Sorrento and Naples and we fell in love. We just knew these would work amazingly with our easy 2-ingredient dough recipe, as the air pocket can be filled with all the traditional Italian meats and cheeses.

## INGREDIENTS

**For the bread**

75g self-raising flour

80g authentic Greek yoghurt

**For the filling**

2 tbsp reduced fat pesto

6 slices of Parma ham

140g light mozzarella

Rocket leaf

## METHOD

Mix the flour and yoghurt together in a bowl to form a dough. Then, split the dough into 2 pieces and roll into balls.

Roll each ball out into an oval shape, about 1cm thick.

Place into a non-stick frying pan and dry fry on a medium-high heat for 2-3 minutes. Then, flip over and cook the other side. When it has puffed up a little to form an air pocket, it's ready.

Remove from the pan and carefully cut open one edge of the bread (be extra careful of the hot steam escaping when you do!).

Fill the bread with the filling and enjoy immediately or pop it into an air fryer or press-style grill to warm through.

## NOTES

The flavour combinations are endless with this one! You can fill it with any type of meat, cheese and vegetables that you like.

# MOUSSAKA

Prep time: 20 minutes | Cooking time: 1 hour and 10 minutes | Serves: 4-6 | Gluten-Free | Calories: 440

Moussaka is one of the most popular Greek dishes, and this version has all the classic flavours! It's great for a hearty family meal but it can also be portioned up, frozen and reheated for lunches, or for those times when you haven't got time to cook.

## INGREDIENTS

Cooking oil spray

2 onions, finely diced

3 cloves of garlic, crushed and chopped

500g 5% fat beef mice

500g 5% fat pork mince

1 x 400g tin of chopped tomatoes

2 tbsp tomato purée

2 tsp nutmeg

2 tsp cinnamon

2 tsp oregano

1 tsp ground black pepper

1 tsp fine sea salt

½ tsp ground clove

3 bay leaves

2 medium potatoes, sliced 2-3mm thick

2 aubergines, sliced 4-5mm thick

**For the topping**

250g cottage cheese

3 eggs

1 tsp nutmeg

60g parmesan

## METHOD

Preheat the oven to 200°c/180°c fan.

Spray a large pan with cooking oil spray and fry the onions and garlic on a medium heat for 3-4 minutes.

Add the beef and pork mince and cook until browned, then add the chopped tomato, tomato purée, dried spices and bay leaves. Simmer for 30 minutes on a medium heat until reduced and thickened.

Meanwhile, cook the potatoes in boiling water until slightly softened. Then, fry the aubergine slices for 2-3 minutes on each side (using a griddle pan if you have one). Set aside.

Once everything is cooked, remove the bay leaves from the mince, and start layering the moussaka in a large baking dish. Start with a layer of potato, then evenly spread a thin layer of the mince mixture, followed by the slices of aubergine (it's okay if they overlap).

Cover with the remaining mince mixture and smooth right up to the edges.

Whisk all the topping ingredients together in a large bowl then spread it evenly on top of the mince.

Place on the middle shelf of the oven and cook for 30 minutes until golden-brown on top.

Remove from the oven and leave to stand for 15 minutes before serving.

# TANDOORI CHICKEN BIRYANI AND BHAJI BAKE

Prep time: 20 minutes | Cooking time: 40 minutes | Serves: 6 | Calories: 463

A beautiful blend of some of our favourite Indian dishes and flavours. This crowd pleaser is perfect for family meals but it's also great for batch cooking and freezing.

## INGREDIENTS

280g basmati rice

600ml cold water

2 bay leaves

1 tsp coriander seeds

3 cardamon pods, split and with the seeds removed

1 tsp turmeric

750g boneless and skinless chicken thighs, chopped

75g fat-free yoghurt

1 tbsp lemon juice

3 tbsp tandoori powder

4 tomatoes, cut into quarters

2 bell peppers, deseeded and cut into chunks

Cooking oil spray

**For the bhaji top**

4 onions, thinly sliced (approx. 350g)

2 sweet potatoes, peeled and grated (approx. 250g)

2 tsp dried coriander leaf

3 tsp garam masala

1 tsp turmeric

Pinch of salt

1 egg

## METHOD

Preheat the oven to 200°c/180°c fan.

Rinse the rice and transfer to a large pan. Add the cold water, bay leaves, coriander seeds, cardamon seeds, and turmeric, stir, then cover the pan with a lid and bring to the boil. Turn down to a simmer for 10-15 minutes or until the water has fully evaporated. Turn off the heat and leave to stand.

Meanwhile, add the chicken to a bowl with the yoghurt, lemon juice and tandoori powder. Mix well and pop to one side. (This can also be prepped in advance and left to marinate in the fridge overnight.)

Place the tomatoes and peppers onto a baking tray, spray with cooking oil, and cook in the oven for 15 minutes.

Then, spray a large frying pan with cooking oil, and cook the chicken over a medium-high heat for 10 minutes. Try to get a little char on the outside of the chicken for extra flavour.

Meanwhile, to make the onion bhaji topping, combine the onion, grated sweet potato, and dried spices in a bowl. Crack in the egg and mix well for 2 minutes before popping to one side.

Remove the bay leaves from the rice, then add the roasted pepper, tomato, and rice to the chicken and stir carefully. Transfer to a baking dish and level out with the back of a spoon.

Top the rice with the onion bhaji mixture, ensuring it's evenly covered. Then, spray the top with cooking oil and place it into the middle shelf of the oven to cook for 25 minutes until nice and golden on top.

## NOTES

You can use chicken breasts instead of thighs or swap them out for more vegetables if you want a totally meat-free version.

# NASI GORENG

Prep time: 10 minutes | Cooking time: 15 minutes | Serves: 2 | Vegetarian, Dairy-Free, Gluten-Free | Calories: 352

Nasi goreng is a very popular Indonesian dish. The translation means 'fried rice', and that's exactly what this dish is. We first tried it in Bali many years ago and we fell in love with it, so we were inspired to make our own healthier version.

## INGREDIENTS

Cooking oil spray

1 onion, finely sliced

2 cloves of garlic, finely chopped

1 carrot, grated

¼ red or white cabbage, shredded

150g cooked white rice

2 tbsp soy sauce

1 tsp red chilli paste

1 egg

1 spring onion, chopped

## METHOD

Heat a large wok or a deep frying pan with a good spray of cooking oil.

Add the onion and garlic and cook for 3-4 minutes until softened, then add the carrot and cabbage and cook for a further 2-3 minutes.

Add the rice, soy sauce and chilli paste and give it a good mix. Fry on a low heat for a further 2-3 minutes.

Meanwhile, in a separate pan, fry an egg.

Serve the fried rice in a bowl and top with the fried egg and chopped spring onions.

## NOTES

This is a vegetarian version, but chicken or prawns could be added to this dish, if desired.

# PERSIAN CHICKEN KEBABS

Prep time: 15 minutes, plus 2-3 hours marinating | Cooking time: 20 minutes | Serves: 2 | Calories: 268

These are also known as 'joojeh kababs' and our version makes a lovely fakeaway dish. Perfect for cooking on the barbecue too! They pack in so much flavour and are such a beautiful colour.

## INGREDIENTS

Pinch of saffron

4 tbsp warm water

2 chicken breasts

1 white onion

2 cloves of garlic

3 tbsp 0% fat Greek yoghurt

3 tbsp lemon juice

1 tsp ground turmeric

1 tsp smoked paprika

## METHOD

Crush the saffron strands in a pestle and mortar to break them down. If you don't have a pestle and mortar, this can be done with the back of a sturdy spoon in a bowl. Add the warm water to the saffron, then set aside for 10 minutes. You should see the water turn a deep yellow colour.

Cut the chicken into chunks and place them into a bowl. Peel the onion and garlic, then grate them into the bowl with the chicken.

Add the yoghurt, lemon juice, turmeric, smoked paprika, and saffron water to the bowl. Mix well, then cover and leave to marinate in the fridge for 2-3 hours if possible.

Remove the chicken from the fridge, then slide the pieces onto your skewers or kebab sticks. Depending on their size, there should be 1 or 2 skewers per person.

Cook the kebabs under the grill for 20 minutes, turning them over halfway through, or cook on the barbecue until fully cooked (10-15 minutes).

## NOTES

This can be prepared the night before and left in the fridge to marinate overnight before cooking.

# SPANISH MEATBALL TOPPED PATATAS BRAVAS

Prep time: 10 minutes | Cooking time: 20 minutes | Serves: 2 | Calories: 450

We had to include a couple of Spanish dishes for our namesake! Here are two classic recipes you'll often see on a tapas menu, but we've combined them to make a delicious, filling meal.

## INGREDIENTS

4 medium potatoes, peeled and cubed

Cooking oil spray

**For the meatballs**

250g 5% fat beef steak mince

1 clove of garlic, crushed and chopped

2 tsp smoked paprika

2 tsp onion granules

½ tsp ground salt

½ tsp black pepper

**For the sauce**

1 x 400g tin of chopped tomatoes

200g passata

1 tsp garlic paste

1 tsp smoked paprika

1 tsp oregano

½ tsp cayenne pepper

2 tbsp red wine vinegar

## METHOD

Spray the potatoes with cooking oil and cook in the air fryer at 170°c for 20 minutes or until cooked through and golden.

Meanwhile, add the meatball ingredients to a bowl and combine. Divide into equal-size balls about 1 inch in diameter.

Spray a large pan with cooking oil and cook the meatballs on a medium-high heat for 10 minutes. Once browned, remove the meatballs and set aside.

Add all the sauce ingredients to the pan and bring to the boil. Then, place the meatballs back into the sauce and turn down to a simmer to cook for 10 minutes.

Pop the cooked potatoes into a bowl and pour the sauce and meatballs over the top to serve.

# SPINACH AND RICOTTA CANNELLONI

Prep time: 10 minutes | Cooking time: 40 minutes | Serves: 2 | Calories: 318

We first had cannelloni in Sorrento—in the very restaurant where the dish was created—and we absolutely loved it.  Spinach and ricotta is an iconic combination and it works great in any pasta dish.

## INGREDIENTS

Cooking oil spray

1 red onion, finely diced

1 clove of garlic, chopped and crushed

Handful fresh basil, finely chopped

800g passata

2 tsp granulated sweetener

300g baby spinach

50ml water

1 egg

250g ricotta

½ tsp nutmeg

20g parmesan, grated

8-10 cannelloni tubes

## METHOD

Preheat the oven to 200°c/180°c fan.

Spray a pan with cooking oil and fry the onion and garlic until softened, then add the fresh basil and stir through.

Pour in the passata and mix, then add the sweetener and leave it to simmer for 10 minutes. Turn off the heat and pop to one side.

Meanwhile, add the spinach and water to a pan on a low heat and cook for 2 minutes until wilted.

Transfer to a sieve and press out as much liquid possible, then chop into small pieces and pop in a bowl. Add the egg, ricotta, nutmeg, and half of the parmesan, and mix well.

Place the mixture into a piping bag and pipe it into each cannelloni tube. (It's easier if you do half into one end of the cannelloni and half into the other.)

Lay the filled pasta in a baking dish and pour the sauce over. Finish with the remaining parmesan and bake in the oven for 25-30 minutes.

Leave to rest for 5 minutes, then serve and enjoy.

# NAVARRO HOME COMFORTS

# CARBONARA

Prep time: 5 minutes | Cooking time: 10 minutes | Serves: 2 | Calories: 465

We love making this one when we need something super quick as it can take as little as 10 minutes. Traditionally, guanciale would be used in this dish, but any cut of pork works equally well.

## INGREDIENTS

150g linguine or spaghetti

3 eggs (1 whole plus 2 yolks)

60g parmesan, grated

½ tsp black pepper

4 rashers of thick bacon, cut into pieces

Fresh parsley, to serve

## METHOD

In a pan of boiling water, cook the pasta for slightly less than the packet instructions so it's al dente.

Drain the pasta water but keep some of it aside for later.

Crack and separate the eggs into a jug then add the parmesan and pepper (reserving a little parmesan to sprinkle over the top to serve). Whisk together and pop to one side.

Fry the chopped bacon in a pan until cooked through, then stir in the cooked pasta.

Take the pan off the heat, then pour in the egg and parmesan mixture, stirring continuously so it coats the pasta fully.

If the sauce is a little too thick, just add a splash of the saved pasta water.

Serve with a sprinkling of chopped fresh parsley and parmesan.

# CHICKEN, CHORIZO AND MUSHROOM RISOTTO

Prep time: 15 minutes | Cooking time: 20 minutes | Serves: 2 | Dairy-Free | Calories: 680

Risotto is a dish we often make when we have ingredients in the fridge that need using up. This is a quick one and uses all those store cupboard staples. Chorizo works well as it releases so much flavour, but you could make this with any meat or vegetables.

## INGREDIENTS

4-6 boneless and skinless chicken thighs

Pinch of salt and pepper

2 tbsp white wine vinegar

Cooking oil spray

600ml chicken stock

2 heaped tsp smoked paprika

5-6 strands of saffron

1 white onion, diced

3 cloves of garlic, finely chopped

8 chestnut mushrooms, roughly chopped

35g chorizo, roughly chopped

160g Arborio risotto rice

## METHOD

Pop the chicken thighs into a large bowl with the salt, pepper, and white wine vinegar. Mix to coat the chicken.

Preheat a large pan with some cooking oil spray in, then add the chicken thighs. Cook for 5-6 minutes, then flip them over to cook for a further 5-6 minutes.

Remove the chicken thighs from the pan (don't wash it up just yet) and chop them into smaller pieces. Pop them to one side for later.

Make the chicken stock in a jug, then add the smoked paprika and saffron, mixing well. Pop this to one side for later.

Using the pan the chicken was cooked in, fry the onion, garlic, mushrooms, and chorizo for 5 minutes. Add the chopped chicken back to the pan.

Stir in the dry risotto rice until all the ingredients are combined. Pour in half of the prepared stock while stirring continuously.

Continue to add the stock a little at a time, making sure you keep stirring constantly until all the stock has been absorbed and the rice is cooked through. This could take 15-20 minutes.

When the rice is tender and has a creamy consistency, divide the risotto between bowls to serve.

## NOTES

The saffron really adds to the flavour of this recipe but if you don't have any it can be left out.

# SWEET CHILLI SALMON AND HALLOUMI SKEWERS

Prep time: 15 minutes | Cooking time: 20 minutes | Serves: 2 | Calories: 655

Salmon and halloumi go so well together, and if you add some sweet chilli sauce it becomes the perfect combination. If you aren't a fish fan, the salmon can easily be swapped out for chicken too!

## INGREDIENTS

180g reduced fat halloumi

4 salmon fillets, skin removed (approx. 150g)

Cooking oil spray

2 tbsp store-bought sweet chilli sauce

**For the homemade sweet chilli sauce**

250g passata

3 tbsp white wine vinegar

2 tbsp lime juice

3 tsp granulated sweetener

2 tsp garlic granules

½ tsp chilli flakes

1 tsp paprika

## METHOD

If using the oven, preheat to 210°c/190°c fan.

Cut each salmon fillet into 3 chunks and cut the halloumi into 8 chunks.

Take 4 skewers and thread 3 salmon chunks and 2 pieces of halloumi onto each.

Spray a baking tray with cooking oil spray and place the skewers on top.

Brush the skewers lightly with store-bought sweet chilli sauce and place into the oven to cook for about 17 minutes. Alternatively, these can be cooked in the air fryer at 180°c for 15 minutes.

Meanwhile, make the homemade sweet chilli sauce by adding all the ingredients to a pan on a medium heat. Cook for 10 minutes until slightly reduced and thickened.

Remove the skewers from the oven and serve with the homemade sweet chilli sauce poured over the top.

## NOTES

We love to serve these on top of flavoured rice, but you could also have them with a flatbread or side salad.

# MEXICAN-STYLE CRISPY CHICKEN BURGER

Prep time: 10 minutes | Cooking time: 25 minutes | Serves: 2 | Gluten-Free* | Calories: 560

Flavoured tortilla chips make a fantastic crispy coating for chicken. This Mexican-style crispy chicken burger is packed with flavour and it's like having a delicious restaurant meal in your own home.

## INGREDIENTS

**For the Mexican spice mix**

1 tsp parsley

1 tsp paprika

1 tsp smoked paprika

1 tsp mild chilli powder

½ tsp cumin

Pinch of pepper

**For the burger**

2 chicken breasts

40g flavoured tortilla chips, plus a few extra for serving  (can be gluten-free*)

1 egg

Cooking oil spray

60g chilli cheddar, grated

2 ciabattas (can be gluten-free*)

Rocket leaf

4 tbsp salsa sauce

## METHOD

If using an oven instead of an air fryer, preheat to 210°c/190°c fan.

Mix the Mexican spice ingredients together in a bowl.

Butterfly the chicken breasts and cut in half so you get 4 thin fillets in total.

In a separate bowl or bag, crush the tortilla chips with a rolling pin to make a crumb. Then, crack the egg into a third bowl and whisk.

Dip each chicken fillet into the spice mix to fully coat, then dip into the egg, and finally coat in the tortilla crumb. Spray with cooking oil spray and place onto a baking tray or into an air fryer.

Cook for 25 minutes in the oven, or for 20 minutes at 180°c in the air fryer until lovely and crispy.

Sprinkle each fillet with the chilli cheddar and heat for a further 1 minute until the cheese has melted.

Serve in the ciabatta with rocket, more tortilla chips and a chunky salsa.

## NOTES

If you prefer things a little spicier, use a hot chilli powder and spicy tortilla chips. Alternatively, if you prefer it milder, swap out the chilli cheese for plain cheddar.

# PORK AND
# CHORIZO PAPPARDELLE

Prep time: 15 minutes | Cooking time: 30 minutes | Serves: 2 | Calories: 595

Pork mince can be quite an underrated ingredient, but if cooked with the right flavours, like in this recipe, it can taste amazing. This recipe is lovely and simple, and it can be ready to serve in about 45 minutes.

## INGREDIENTS

Cooking oil spray

1 onion, diced

2 cloves of garlic, finely chopped

250g 5% fat pork mince

50g chorizo, diced

2 tbsp red wine vinegar

3 tbsp tomato purée

1 carrot, grated

200ml chicken stock

400g chopped tomatoes

1 tsp thyme

1 tsp basil

Pinch of salt

2 bay leaves

150g pappardelle

Parmesan, to serve

## METHOD

Heat some cooking oil spray in a large pan, then add the onion and garlic and fry for 2-3 minutes.

Add the pork mince and chorizo and fry for 10 minutes. When cooked through, stir in the red wine vinegar, tomato purée, and grated carrot and fry for 5 minutes more.

Pour in the chicken stock and chopped tomatoes, then stir in the thyme, basil, salt, and bay leaves.

Reduce the heat to low and leave to simmer for 15 minutes to reduce.

Meanwhile, cook the pappardelle as per the packet instructions. Once cooked, drain and stir into the ragu.

Portion into two bowls and top with a shaving of parmesan.

## NOTES

This dish can be made with any pasta of your choice.

# ROAST POTATO TOPPED COTTAGE PIE

Prep time: 20 minutes | Cooking time: 1 hour 25 minutes | Serves: 4 | Dairy-Free, Gluten-Free | Calories: 565

The traditional cottage pie with a twist, and a perfect family meal! We created this recipe as Zoe isn't a fan of mashed potato but loves roast potatoes. The crispiness of the potatoes with the rich beef mince work really well together. This also makes delicious leftovers when reheated.

## INGREDIENTS

8 medium potatoes, chopped into chunks

Cooking oil spray

2 white onions, chopped

1 clove of garlic, crushed

500g 5% fat beef mince

1 beef stock pot

1 tsp English mustard

1 tbsp tomato purée

4 tbsp Worcestershire sauce or Henderson's Relish

700ml beef stock

1 tsp celery salt

1 tsp thyme

3 carrots, finely diced

100g garden peas

3 bay leaves

3 tbsp beef gravy granules

## METHOD

Preheat the oven to 190°c/170°c fan. Place the potatoes into a pan of water and bring to the boil. Cook until they begin to soften slightly.

Drain the potatoes and then transfer them onto a roasting tray. Spray them with oil and place in the oven to roast for approximately 30 minutes.

Meanwhile, in a large pan, fry the onion in one or two sprays of oil for 2-3 minutes. Add the garlic and beef mince, mix well and cook until the mince browns.

Stir in the stock pot, mustard, tomato purée, and Worcestershire sauce or Henderson's Relish. Mix well until the ingredients are combined.

Make the beef stock in a jug and stir in the celery salt and thyme, then pour it into the pan.

Add the carrots, peas, and bay leaves to the pan. Mix well until combined and leave to simmer on a low heat for 30 minutes until the sauce has reduced.

Stir in the beef gravy granules and mix well, then simmer for a further 5 minutes.

Transfer the beef mixture to a large baking dish and smooth the surface to make it level. Remove the potatoes from the oven, then arrange them on top of the mince.

Spray the potatoes once more with oil and place the dish into the oven to bake for 10 minutes, then remove and leave to rest for 10 minutes before serving.

### NOTES
This recipe could be made vegetarian by swapping out the mince for a meat-free alternative, using vegetable stock and gravy granules instead of beef, and adding Henderson's Relish instead of Worcestershire sauce.

# CLASSIC BOLOGNESE RAGU

Prep time: 10 minutes | Cooking time: 40 minutes | Serves: 2 | Dairy-Free, Gluten-Free | Calories: 405

Bolognese Ragu is one of those classic dishes. It's usually served with pasta, but it's so versatile that it can be used in loads of dishes. We often make a large batch so we can either eat it over a few nights or pop some in the freezer for later.

## INGREDIENTS

Cooking oil spray

1 large onion, diced

2 cloves of garlic, finely chopped

500g 5% fat beef steak mince

2 tbsp tomato purée

1 x 400g tin of chopped tomatoes

1 medium carrot, grated

1 tsp celery salt

1 tsp Italian mixed herbs

3 bay leaves

2 tbsp red wine vinegar

## METHOD

Spray a large pan with cooking spray and fry the onion and garlic for 3-5 minutes or until the onion has softened.

Add the minced beef and cook for 2-3 minutes or until browned.

Add the tomato purée and mix through, then add the tinned tomatoes and bring to the boil.

Add the grated carrot, celery salt, Italian mixed herbs, bay leaves and red wine vinegar. Cover with a lid and simmer for 30-40 minutes until the sauce has reduced.

Season to taste with salt and pepper, serve immediately, or leave to cool, portion up and freeze for later.

# COFFEE BRAISED
# BEEF BRISKET

Prep time: 10 minutes | Cooking time: 6 hours 30 minutes | Serves: 4 | Calories: 390

We both absolutely love a good coffee, so we knew we had to incorporate it into a recipe, and with one of our favourite cuts of meat too! This one's a bit of a Sunday special and a real crowd pleaser. It takes a little longer to prepare, but once in the oven it can be left for hours to cook slowly, and it's so worth the wait!

## INGREDIENTS

1-1.5kg beef brisket joint

1 onion, sliced

2 carrots, peeled and sliced

600ml beef stock

2 tsp beef gravy granules (optional)

**For the brisket rub**

15g ground coffee

1 tbsp garlic granules

2 tbsp granulated sweetener

2 tsp smoked paprika

1 tsp fine sea salt

1 tsp parsley

You will need a roasting tray with a raised rack for this recipe.

## METHOD

Preheat the oven to 200°c/180°c fan.

Mix the rub ingredients together and sprinkle over the whole of the brisket joint. Rub in so it's fully covered, then pop to one side.

Place the onion and carrots in a roasting tray and cover with the beef stock.

Place the rack into the tray and sit the brisket on top, then pop into the middle of the oven and cook for 30 minutes, uncovered.

Remove from the oven and place a sheet of greaseproof paper over the meat (this will stop the foil from sticking to it), then cover with foil and seal around the edges to keep all the heat and moisture locked in. Pop back in the oven and turn the heat down to 145°c/125°c fan.

Cook for 4 hours, then remove the meat and place on a large sheet of foil. Spoon over 4-5 tablespoons of cooking juices from the tray and then wrap the meat tightly. Double up the foil if required to stop any moisture from escaping. Set the onion, carrot, and remaining cooking juices aside.

Place the brisket on an ovenproof tray and pop back in the oven for 2 hours more.

When it's finished cooking, remove the meat and let it rest for a minimum of 15 minutes in the foil before shredded or carving.

Transfer the onion, carrot and leftover liquid to a measuring jug and top up to a pint with water.

Using a hand blender or food processer, blend to a smooth gravy.

Add the gravy to a saucepan and bring to the boil (you can add a couple of teaspoons of beef gravy granules to thicken, if desired). Once the gravy has reduced, serve alongside the shredded brisket, roasted potatoes and vegetables.

# CREAMY GARLIC CHICKEN

Prep time: 10 minutes | Cooking time: 25 minutes | Serves: 2 | Gluten-Free | Calories: 490

Juicy chicken thighs in a creamy garlic and mushroom sauce. This dish feels like a real treat, but it's cooked in under 30 minutes, so it's perfect for a midweek meal.

## INGREDIENTS

6 boneless and skinless chicken thighs

2 tbsp lemon juice

1 tsp paprika

1 tsp oregano

1 tsp thyme

Cooking oil spray

1 white onion, finely sliced

100g mushrooms, sliced

4 cloves of garlic, roughly chopped

250ml semi-skimmed milk

Good pinch of fresh parsley, chopped

2 tbsp cornflour, mixed with 2 tbsp water

## METHOD

Place the chicken thighs in a bowl with the lemon juice, paprika, oregano and thyme, and mix until the chicken is fully coated.

Place a skillet or large frying pan on a medium heat and spray with cooking oil spray. Add the chicken and cook for approximately 10 minutes until cooked through and slightly browned.

Remove the chicken from the pan and set aside, then add the onion, mushrooms and garlic to the same pan and fry until softened.

Add the milk and fresh parsley and leave to simmer for 10 minutes.

Add the cornflour mix, stirring continuously until the sauce thickens.

Return the chicken to the pan and warm through before serving with a side of rice.

# SLOW COOKER BEEF BOURGUIGNON

Prep time: 30 minutes | Cooking time: 4-5 hours | Serves: 4 | Dairy-Free, Gluten-Free | Calories: 330

This is the ultimate comfort slow cooker meal! A rich and hearty beef stew that's a healthier take on the classic French bourguignon. A fabulous recipe to feed a family (but a great one for leftovers, too!).

## INGREDIENTS

500g lean diced beef

6 rashers of bacon, chopped and the fat removed

10 small shallots, peeled

2 cloves of garlic, chopped

3 carrots, chopped

250ml red wine

250ml beef stock

2 tsp thyme

2 tbsp tomato purée

2 tbsp cornflour, mixed with 2 tbsp water

## METHOD

Brown the beef in a frying pan for 3-4 minutes to seal in the flavour, then transfer to the slow cooker.

In the same pan, add the chopped bacon, shallots, garlic and carrot and fry for 3-4 minutes before transferring to the slow cooker.

Return the pan to the heat and pour in the red wine (it should sizzle). Scrape the bottom of the pan with a wooden spoon to deglaze it and collect all the flavour.

Add the wine to the slow cooker along with the beef stock, tomato purée and thyme. Place the lid on and leave to cook on medium for 4-5 hours or until the beef is tender.

Remove the lid and add the cornflour mix, stirring until the sauce has thickened slightly.

Leave uncovered for a further 10 minutes before serving.

### NOTES

If using a multi-cooker, the frying steps of this recipe can be done in there before switching to slow cooker mode.

# MASALA FISH CAKES

Prep time: 15 minutes, plus 2 hours refrigeration | Cooking time: 40 minutes | Serves: 4 | Calories: 335

These Indian-inspired fish cakes have a fluffy spiced potato filling and a crispy coating. They're perfect as a main meal or could be made smaller and served as a snack or as part of a buffet.

## INGREDIENTS

3 medium potatoes

2 salmon fillets (approx. 400g)

1 tbsp lemon juice

1 tsp coriander, freshly chopped, or 1 tsp dried coriander leaf

½ tsp turmeric

½ tsp cumin

2 cloves of garlic, crushed

2 spring onions, chopped

1 red chilli, finely diced

1 tsp fine sea salt

1 tsp garam masala

½ tsp ground coriander

4 small slices wholemeal bread

1 medium egg

Cooking oil spray

## METHOD

Preheat the oven to 200°c/180°c fan.

Peel and chop the potatoes and par boil them for 10 minutes until slightly softened.

Coat the salmon fillets in the lemon juice, then wrap them in foil and cook in the oven for 20 minutes.

Drain the potatoes, then add the coriander, turmeric, cumin, garlic, spring onions, chilli, sea salt, garam masala, and ground coriander, and mash together. Set aside and allow to cool.

When the salmon has cooked, remove from the oven and carefully break it into flakes with the back of a fork. Fold the salmon into the mashed potato, being careful not to over-mix it.

Split the mixture into 4 portions and shape them into patties, then place them onto a tray and cover. Allow to rest in the fridge overnight or for a minimum of 2 hours.

To make the breadcrumbs, first toast the slices of bread. Once cooled, add them to a food blender and blend to a coarse crumb. Then, pour the crumbs into a large bowl.

Whisk the egg in a bowl and dip each fish cake into the egg and then into the breadcrumbs, making sure to cover each cake fully.

Spray a large frying pan with cooking oil spray and fry the fish cakes for 5 minutes on each side over a medium heat.

Remove from the frying pan, place on an ovenproof tray, and cook for a further 15 minutes in a preheated oven at 200°c/180°c fan until they're piping hot in the middle. Alternatively, you can cook them in an air fryer at 180°c for 20 minutes or until golden brown.

## NOTES

We love to serve these with our Kachumber Salad (see page 178) and raita.

# STEAK DIANE

Prep time: 15 minutes | Cooking time: 15 minutes | Serves: 2 | Calories: 340

A classic steak dish made with a creamy mushroom sauce. It's perfect for a special occasion or a date night, but quick and easy enough for a midweek meal too.

## INGREDIENTS

Cooking oil spray

1 small onion, finely chopped

4 white button mushrooms, sliced

1 clove of garlic, finely chopped

½ beef stock cube

40ml water

2 beef steaks (rump or sirloin work well)

½ tsp mustard powder

2 heaped tbsp fat-free natural yoghurt

## METHOD

Heat some cooking oil spray in a large frying pan, then add the chopped onion and cook for 2-3 minutes until softened.

In the same pan, add the chopped mushroom and garlic and cook for a further 2-3 minutes until softened.

Turn the heat to high, crumble in the beef stock cube, add the water, and simmer for 5 minutes.

Meanwhile, in a separate pan, cook the steaks to your liking.

Add the mustard powder to the mushrooms and season to taste.

Remove the sauce from the heat and add the natural yoghurt, stirring continuously until heated through. Serve immediately on top of the steaks.

## NOTES

Serve on a bed of mashed potatoes with a side of tenderstem broccoli.

# SMASH BURGERS

Prep time: 10 minutes | Cooking time: 5 minutes | Serves: 2 | Calories: 550

Smash burgers are on the top of our list when it comes to the ultimate fakeaway meals. They only need a couple of ingredients and take just 15 minutes to make. The method of smashing the burger thinly and cooking it quickly gives it a lovely tender texture and a wonderfully crisp edge.

## INGREDIENTS

400g 5% beef steak mince

Cooking oil spray

Pinch of sea salt

Reduced fat cheese slices

**To serve**

2 brioche buns, lightly toasted

Burger sauce

Salad leaves

Red onion, sliced

Tomato, sliced

## METHOD

Split the mince into 6 equal portions and roll into balls.

Spray a large frying pan with cooking oil and place on a high heat. When it's hot and starts to smoke slightly, put a meatball in the centre of the frying pan with a square of greaseproof paper over the top.

Press down using a burger press or the base of a small pan and hold for 10 seconds, squashing the meatball flat to create the smashed burger patty.

Move to the side of the pan and repeat with the remaining meatballs (but try not to overcrowd the pan as it'll bring the heat down).

Once the burgers have caramelised on the bottom, about 2-3 minutes, flip and press down again with a spatula. Cook for a further 2 minutes or until both sides are caramelised and crispy, then sprinkle with a pinch of salt to season.

Add a cheese slice to each patty and stack 3 on top of each other. Then, layer the brioche buns with the burger stack followed by the burger sauce, salad leaf, sliced red onion and tomato.

Enjoy with crispy fries topped with chip spice.

# HUNTER'S PASTA BAKE

Prep time: 10 minutes | Cooking time: 30 minutes | Serves: 4 | Calories: 570

A twist on the classic Hunter's Chicken! The combination of chicken, BBQ sauce, bacon and cheese with pasta makes for a delicious hearty meal that all the family will love.

## INGREDIENTS

300g dried pasta (fusilli works well)

8 rashers of bacon, fat removed

250g cooked chicken, diced

160g grated mozzarella

**For the BBQ sauce**

1 x 400g tin of chopped tomatoes

1 x 500g carton of passata

3 tbsp tomato purée

4 tbsp balsamic vinegar

3 tbsp Worcestershire sauce or Henderson's Relish

2 cloves of garlic, crushed, or 2 tsp garlic paste

2 tsp granulated sweetener

3 tsp smoked paprika

1½ tsp mustard powder

1 tsp onion granules

## METHOD

Preheat the oven to 210°c/190°c fan.

Cook the pasta for 2 minutes less than the packet instructions until al dente. Drain, then set aside.

Meanwhile, add all the BBQ sauce ingredients to a large pan and simmer on a medium heat for 10 minutes until reduced and thickened.

Pan or air fry the bacon until cooked through. Then, cut 6 of the rashers into 6 or 8 pieces each and add to the BBQ sauce. Cut the other 2 pieces of bacon into smaller bits and fry again until crispy.

Add the cooked chicken and drained pasta into the BBQ sauce and stir to combine. Stir through half of the grated mozzarella then transfer the mixture to a large baking dish.

Sprinkle the remaining mozzarella over the top and finish with the crispy bacon bits. Then, place the dish into the centre of the oven and cook for 20 minutes.

Remove from the oven and leave to stand for 5-10 minutes before serving with a side salad and slice of garlic bread.

## NOTES

We love making this recipe for the two of us and having the leftovers at work the next day. It freezes well and can be reheated in the microwave or oven.

# FRENCH ONION BEEF STROGANOFF

Prep time: 15 minutes | Cooking time: 25 minutes | Serves: 2 | Calories: 632

A delicious one pot meal that combines the classic flavours of beef and mushroom stroganoff with French onion soup. It's so beautifully creamy and cheesy; we love this hearty and filling dish.

## INGREDIENTS

Cooking oil spray

2 sirloin or rump steaks

2 onions, thinly sliced

3 tbsp red wine vinegar

70g mushrooms, sliced

3 cloves of garlic, crushed and chopped

400ml beef stock

1 tsp thyme

1 tsp dill

2 tbsp Worcestershire sauce or Henderson's Relish

150g dried noodles

250g fat-free fromage frais

80g light cheddar, grated

## METHOD

Preheat the grill or an oven to 190°c/170°c fan.

Add cooking oil spray to a large frying or cast-iron pan and fry the steak for approximately 3 minutes on each side. Remove from the pan and leave to rest.

In the same pan, add the sliced onion and fry for 2-3 minutes. Pour in the red wine vinegar and deglaze the pan.

Add the mushroom and garlic and fry for a further minute before adding the beef stock, thyme, dill, and Worcestershire sauce. Bring to a boil.

Turn down to a low heat and add the noodles, then leave to simmer for 10 minutes or until the noodles have cooked through and the broth has reduced.

Slice or chop the steaks, add to the pan, and warm through.

Remove the pan from the heat and stir in the fromage frais. Then, sprinkle with grated cheese and pop under a grill or in the oven until melted and bubbling.

## NOTES

The fromage frais can be substituted for crème fraiche or quark.

# SLOW COOKER MOROCCAN LAMB TAGINE

Prep time: 10 minutes | Cooking time: 6 hours 10 minutes | Serves: 4 | Calories: 470

A hearty and flavoursome slow cooker recipe that's super easy to prepare and can be left to cook for hours. Walking into the kitchen after it's been cooking all day and smelling the Moroccan spices and aromas is just incredible!

## INGREDIENTS

Cooking oil spray

600g lean lamb leg or shoulder steak, diced

1 onion, chopped

2 cloves of garlic, chopped

2 carrots, chopped

300ml lamb or chicken stock

1 x 400g tin of chopped tomatoes

1 x 400g tin of chickpeas, drained

240g dried apricots

2 tsp ras el hanout

2 tsp allspice

2 tsp paprika

1 cinnamon stick

3 bay leaves

## METHOD

Set the slow cooker to a low heat, then spray a frying pan with cooking oil spray and brown the lamb before transferring it to the slow cooker.

Add the onion and garlic to the pan and fry for a few minutes until softened and slightly browned, then transfer to the slow cooker.

Add the remaining ingredients to the slow cooker and stir through, then pop the lid on and cook for about 6 hours.

Remove the cinnamon stick and bay leaves before serving.

### NOTES

We love to serve this with couscous and our Easy Flatbreads (see page 172).

# LASAGNE
# STUFFED PEPPERS

Prep time: 10 minutes | Cooking time: 30 minutes | Serves: 2 | Gluten-Free | Calories: 550

A beautiful twist on both stuffed pepper and lasagne, and a great one to make if you have leftover bolognese!
This recipe makes four stuffed peppers, so it's perfect for a main meal for two, or it can serve 4 as a small lunch or side dish.

## INGREDIENTS

4 large red or yellow peppers

6 slices prosciutto, cut in half, plus 1 for garnish

Classic Bolognese Ragu (see page 94)

180g ricotta, divided into 4 equal portions

80g light mozzarella, grated

## METHOD

Carefully cut the tops off the peppers, then scoop out the white parts and remove the seeds. You might need to cut a little off the bottom so that they stand upright but be careful not to make a hole.

Place the peppers in the air fryer tray, spray with cooking oil, and sprinkle with a pinch of salt.

Cook for 12 minutes at 180°c until slightly softened.

Add a slice of prosciutto to the bottom of each pepper, then add a layer of bolognese and ricotta. Repeat these layers until all ingredients have been used up and the peppers are filled to the top.

Top each pepper with 20g of grated mozzarella, then pop back into the air fryer to cook for a further 15 minutes.

Dice the final slice of prosciutto and fry in a pan until crispy.

Once the peppers have cooked, sprinkle the crispy prosciutto over the top and serve.

## NOTES

These could be made vegetarian by using meat-free alternatives. They can also be cooked in the oven at 210°c /190°c fan following the same timings.

# KEEMA CURRY

Prep time: 10 minutes | Cooking time: 45 minutes | Serves: 4 | Dairy-Free, Gluten-Free | Calories: 274

Keema, in Indian cooking, refers to minced meat, which is the main ingredient of this dish. This recipe is packed with flavour, uses all the store cupboard staples, and is perfect for a midweek meal.

## INGREDIENTS

Cooking oil spray

1 onion, finely chopped

3 cloves of garlic, finely chopped

500g 5% fat beef mince

1 carrot, finely diced

1 tbsp cumin seeds

1 tsp ground ginger

½ tsp ground cloves

2 tsp coriander

2 tsp garam masala

1 tsp turmeric

½ tsp ground cinnamon

1 green chilli, chopped (add more for extra heat)

3 tsp tomato purée

2 x 400g tins of chopped tomatoes

300ml chicken stock

2 bay leaves

100g frozen peas

Coriander leaves, chopped, to serve

## METHOD

Heat a large pan with cooking oil spray and add the onion and garlic. Sauté for 5 minutes until softened.

Add the beef mince and carrot and fry for 3-5 minutes until the mince has browned.

Stir in the dried spices, green chilli, and tomato purée, then cook for a further 5 minutes, stirring continuously.

Add the tinned tomatoes, chicken stock, and bay leaves, and stir through. Cover the pan with a lid and turn down to a simmer for 25 minutes.

Remove the pan lid, add the peas, and cook for a further 5 minutes.

Remove the bay leaves, garnish with fresh coriander leaves, and serve with rice and naan.

## NOTES

Try adapting our Easy Flatbreads recipe (see page 172) to make your own homemade naan.

# BAKED
# ENCHILADA

Prep time: 10 minutes | Cooking time: 40 minutes | Serves: 2 | Calories: 530

This is one of the first recipes we made a healthier version of when we started our weight-loss journey, and it's still one of our favourites today. It's just as tasty and has all the flavours of one you would get in a Mexican restaurant.

## INGREDIENTS

Cooking oil spray

1 onion, chopped

2 bell peppers, chopped

1 clove of garlic, finely chopped

2 chicken breasts or 6 chicken thigh fillets, diced

2 tsp smoked paprika

1 tsp hot paprika

½ tsp chilli flakes

1 tsp garlic granules

2 tsp mixed herbs

Pinch of salt and pepper

1 x 400g tin of chopped tomatoes

200g passata

2 tbsp tomato purée

2 tbsp balsamic vinegar

2 tortilla wraps

80g reduced fat cheddar, grated

## METHOD

Preheat the oven to 210°c/190°c fan.

Spray a large pan with cooking oil and fry the onion, pepper, and garlic for 5 minutes until softened. Remove from the pan and set aside.

Add the chicken to the same pan and fry for 2-3 minutes until it browns at the edges.

Add the smoked paprika, hot paprika, chilli flakes, garlic granules, mixed herbs, a pinch of salt and pepper, and stir through. Then, add the onions, garlic, and pepper back to the pan.

Add the chopped tomatoes, passata, tomato purée and balsamic vinegar. Stir, then simmer on a low heat for about 20 minutes until the sauce has reduced and thickened slightly.

Take two single-serve baking dishes and lay a wrap in each. Place the chicken and tomato mixture on the top, leaving some of the liquid sauce in the pan.

Fold the sides of the wrap over, then pour the remaining sauce over the top. This will hold the sides closed.

Sprinkle the grated cheddar over the top and cook in the oven for 15 minutes.

## NOTES

This can be made vegetarian by swapping the chicken for a meat-free alternative, beans, or vegetables.

# HONEY CHEERIO
# CHICKEN TENDERS

Prep time: 10 minutes | Cooking time: 20 minutes | Serves: 2 | Dairy-Free | Calories: 360

This is our absolute favourite way to coat crispy chicken - for us, it beats breadcrumbs any day. The honey cereal gives it that slight sweetness and makes it super crispy, but keeps it juicy and tender on the inside.

## INGREDIENTS

80g Honey Cheerios (or any honey-flavoured hoop cereal)

2 chicken breasts, cut into strips

1 egg

Cooking oil spray

## METHOD

Blitz the honey cereal in a food processor to make a fine crumb, then pop it into a bowl. Crack and whisk the egg into a separate bowl.

Dip each piece of chicken into the crumb, then into the egg, then back into the crumb. Dipping into the crumb helps the egg to stick, and then the double crumb makes it super crispy!

Place into an air fryer tray and spray with cooking oil spray.

Cook for around 20 minutes at 170°c or until crispy and golden.

## NOTES

We love to have these as a main meal with fries, salad and dipping sauces, but they can also be made for sharing or snacking.

# BEEF
# KUNG PAO

Prep time: 10 minutes | Cooking time: 25 minutes | Serves: 2-3 | Dairy-Free, Gluten-Free, Contains Nuts | Calories: 390

A sweet and slightly spicy dish that is packed with flavour. This healthier, home-cooked version of the popular Chinese takeaway dish is super easy to make and can be cooked in one pan!

## INGREDIENTS

20g peanuts

2 beef steaks (sirloin works well)

3 spring onions, chopped

1 red chilli, deseeded and chopped

2 cloves of garlic, finely chopped

2cm fresh ginger, cut into matchsticks

⅓ red pepper, chopped

⅓ yellow pepper, chopped

2 tbsp apple cider vinegar

2 tbsp dark soy sauce

## METHOD

In a large frying pan or wok, dry roast the peanuts on a high heat for 3 minutes and set aside.

Cook the steaks to a medium rare, around 3-4 minutes either side, remove from the heat, and leave to rest.

Stir fry half the spring onions, half the chilli, and all the garlic and ginger for 5 minutes.

Add the peppers, stir, and cook for a further 5 minutes.

Slice the steak and add it back to the pan.

Add the cider vinegar and soy sauce, stir, and cook for 5 minutes.

Take the pan off the heat, stir the peanuts through, and season with salt and pepper.

Serve with basmati rice and top with the remaining chilli and spring onion.

## NOTES

This dish could also be made with chicken, or you could use a meat-free alternative to make it vegetarian.

# BAKED HUNTER'S CHICKEN

Prep time: 25 minutes | Cooking time: 30 minutes | Serves: 2 | Gluten-Free | Calories: 475

One of the great British pub grub classics but made healthier at home! This is a fab midweek meal and one that all the family will love, too!

## INGREDIENTS

2 chicken breasts

1 clove of garlic, crushed and chopped

3 tbsp tomato purée

½ tsp mustard powder

1 tsp smoked paprika

2 tbsp apple cider vinegar

200ml passata

5 tbsp Worcestershire sauce or Henderson's Relish

5 tbsp balsamic vinegar

1 tsp granulated sweetener

1 onion, chopped

1 bell pepper, chopped

4 rashers of bacon, fat removed

80g mozzarella or light cheddar, grated

## METHOD

Preheat the oven to 200°c/180°c fan.

Wrap the chicken breasts in foil, place on an ovenproof tray and cook for 20 minutes.

While the chicken is cooking, make the BBQ sauce. Cook the garlic on a medium heat for 2 minutes, then add the tomato purée, mustard powder, smoked paprika and apple cider vinegar. Stir though and cook for 1 minute.

Add the passata, Worcestershire sauce (or Henderson's Relish), balsamic vinegar and sweetener. Bring to the boil, then turn down to a simmer.

Add the pepper and onion to a separate frying pan with a little cooking oil spray. Fry for 5-10 minutes until softened, then turn off the heat.

Remove the chicken from the oven and separate into two ovenproof dishes.

Divide the onions and peppers between the dishes, then wrap two slices of bacon over the top of each chicken breast.

Pour BBQ sauce over the chicken breasts so they're fully covered, then sprinkle each dish with half the cheese and bake in the oven for 15 minutes.

## NOTES

To serve 4, double the recipe. This can be cooked in a large baking dish and then served individually.

# CAJUN CHEESESTEAK FLATBREADS

Prep time: 5 minutes | Cooking time: 15 minutes | Serves: 1 | Calories: 455

Cheesesteak is an American classic that's typically served in baguette-style bread, but we love folded flatbreads so use them to give this recipe a little twist. The addition of the Cajun rub gives it an extra hint of spice, too.

## INGREDIENTS

1 beef steak (rump or sirloin work well)

1 folded flatbread

35g squeezy cheese (we use Primula)

**For the Cajun spice mix**

1 tsp paprika

1 tsp smoked paprika

1 tsp garlic granules

½ tsp oregano

½ tsp thyme

½ tsp cayenne pepper

Pinch of salt and pepper

## METHOD

Preheat the oven to 200°c/180°c fan.

Combine the Cajun spice mix ingredients in a bowl then rub the steak with the spice mix so that it's fully coated.

Heat a frying or griddle pan until red hot, then add the steak and cook to your liking. For a thicker steak, we recommend cooking for about 5 minutes on both sides, but cooking timings vary depending on the thickness of steak and how well done you prefer it.

Place the flatbread onto a baking tray, then cut the steak into slices and layer this in the folded flatbread with the squeezy cheese.

Pop into the oven for 5 minutes to heat through and allow the cheese to melt.

## NOTES

If you prefer, you can use a pre-made Cajun spice mix. Or you could even use our Easy Flatbread recipe (see page 172) to make the whole dish homemade!

# AWESOME
# SAUCES

# CARAMELISED ONION HUMMUS

Prep time: 5 minutes | Cooking time: 10 minutes | Serves: 6 | Vegetarian, Gluten-Free | Calories: 66

We've given our classic hummus a little lift with this recipe. The addition of the sweet, homemade caramelised onion makes this one an absolute treat. Serve with crudités and warm flatbreads or pittas.

## INGREDIENTS

Cooking oil spray

1 red onion, finely chopped

2 tsp granulated sweetener

1 x 400g tin of chickpeas

2 tbsp 0% fat Greek yoghurt

1 clove of garlic, chopped

2 tbsp lemon juice

½ tsp ground cumin

Pinch of salt

## METHOD

Spray a pan with cooking oil spray and fry the onion on low for 5-7 minutes until softened. Leave the lid on and add a couple of tablespoons of water halfway through. The lid will keep moisture in the pan and allow the onion to sauté and fully soften without browning.

Add the sweetener and mix, cooking for a further minute before removing from the heat. Pop to one side and leave to cool.

Drain and rinse the chickpeas, saving some of the chickpea water to use later, if required.

Add the chickpeas, yoghurt, garlic, lemon juice, cumin, and salt to a blender and pulse until completely smooth (or to your desired consistency). If it needs thinning slightly, add a couple of tablespoons of chickpea water.

Add the caramelised onion, making sure you get all the flavour from the pan, then pulse until the onion is combined.

Serve and enjoy.

# RED
# PEPPER DIP

Prep time: 10 minutes | Cooking time: 20 minutes | Serves: 2 | Vegetarian, Gluten-Free, Dairy-Free | Calories: 64

This dish is a famous favourite, so we just had to create our own healthier version. This versatile recipe is perfect as a side, a snack for dipping, part of a packed lunch, or on a buffet or grazing table.

## INGREDIENTS

2 red peppers, chopped into large chunks

1 large tomato, quartered and deseeded

1 small red onion, peeled and quartered

1 clove of garlic, peeled

Cooking oil spray

2 tbsp balsamic vinegar

1 tbsp red wine vinegar

## METHOD

Preheat the oven to 190°c/170°c fan.

Place the pepper, tomato, onion, and garlic into an ovenproof dish and spray with oil.

Roast in the oven for approximately 20 minutes, or until the vegetables start to char.

Remove the dish from the oven and leave to cool slightly for 5 minutes.

Add the roasted vegetables to a blender along with the balsamic vinegar and red wine vinegar.

Blitz the mixture until smooth, with a few chunks remaining (or blitz to your preferred texture).

## NOTES

Instead of being roasted in the oven, the vegetables can also be cooked in the air fryer at 190°c for 15 minutes.

# TZATZIKI

Prep time: 10 minutes | Serves: 4 | Vegetarian, Gluten-Free | Calories: 68

A beautifully simple Greek recipe and one of the first we made a healthier version of. We love having tzatziki with pitta bread, or with some of our favourite Greek meals, such as our Chicken Gyros (see page 62) or souvlaki.

## INGREDIENTS

400g authentic Greek yoghurt

2 cloves of garlic, crushed and finely chopped

10cm cucumber

1 lemon, juiced, or 2 tbsp lemon juice

Fresh dill tips, chopped, or 1 tsp dried dill

## METHOD

Place the yoghurt into a bowl and stir in the chopped garlic.

Stand the cucumber on its end and carefully slice down the sides from top to bottom to remove the skin, cutting about 2mm in. Then, take each section of skin and slice in half lengthways before turning widthways and chopping into small pieces.

Add the cucumber skin, lemon juice, and dill to the yoghurt and mix well.

## NOTES

To save any wastage, use the leftover cucumber flesh to make a delicious Greek-style salad.

# SOUR CREAM

Prep time: 5 minutes | Serves: 4 | Vegetarian, Gluten-Free | Calories: 13

A deliciously simple dip recipe. This one is great paired with Mexican-style food, something with a little spice, or served alongside crudités. It works well with both fresh and cupboard ingredients.

## INGREDIENTS

3 tbsp fat-free fromage frais

½ lemon, juiced, or 2 tbsp lemon juice

1 clove of garlic, crushed, or 1 tsp garlic granules

Small handful fresh chives, chopped, or ½ tsp dried chives

## METHOD

Add all the ingredients to a bowl and stir well until combined.

## NOTES

If fat-free fromage frais is unavailable, 0% fat Greek yoghurt works well too.

# BACONNAISE

Prep time: 10 minutes | Cooking time: 10 minutes | Serves: 3-4 | Gluten-Free | Calories: 34

A bacon-flavoured mayonnaise or, in this case, a healthier alternative to mayonnaise that tastes just as good! It has a subtle smoky flavour and goes great with burgers or as a dip with chips.

## INGREDIENTS

3 rashers of bacon, fat removed

Cooking oil spray

3 tbsp 0% fat Greek yoghurt

1 tbsp lemon juice

½ tsp sweet paprika

½ tsp smoked paprika

½ tsp garlic granules

## METHOD

Chop the bacon into small pieces and add to a preheated, oiled frying pan. Fry until crispy, then remove and place onto a sheet of kitchen towel to cool. Meanwhile, mix the yoghurt, lemon juice, sweet and smoked paprika and garlic granules together in a bowl.

Chop the crispy bacon into smaller pieces, add to the yoghurt mix, and stir to combine.

## NOTES

If serving as a dip on its own, save a few pieces of crispy bacon to serve on top as decoration.

# SMOKY BBQ SAUCE

Prep time: 5 minutes | Cooking time: 10 minutes | Serves: 6 | Vegetarian, Dairy-Free, Gluten-Free | Calories: 22

A sweet and smoky BBQ sauce that can be used for the base of many dishes or served as a dipping sauce.

## INGREDIENTS

400g passata

1 clove of garlic, crushed and chopped

3 tbsp tomato purée

4 tbsp balsamic vinegar

2 tsp granulated sweetener

3 tsp smoked paprika

1 tsp mustard powder

½ tsp cayenne pepper

## METHOD

Add all the ingredients to a saucepan on a medium heat and bring to the boil.

Turn down to a simmer and cook for 5-10 minutes until reduced and thickened slightly.

# TARTARE SAUCE

Prep time: 10 minutes | Serves: 4 | Vegetarian, Gluten-Free, Dairy-Free | Calories: 25

The traditional accompaniment to good old fish and chips! We often make our own chippy tea at home, so we created this recipe to go alongside it for the most authentic experience.

## INGREDIENTS

2 tbsp light mayonnaise

1 tsp capers, finely chopped

3 mini gherkins, finely diced

¼ small red onion, very finely chopped

4 tbsp pickling vinegar (from the jarred capers or gherkins)

1 tsp fresh or dried dill

## METHOD

Add all the ingredients into a bowl and mix well.

Serve immediately or store in the fridge for up to 10 days.

## NOTES

You can also use normal mayonnaise or lighter than light, if preferred.

# HOLIDAY HEROES

# FESTIVE TURKEY AND CRANBERRY SCOTCH EGG

Prep time: 30 minutes | Cooking time: 30 minutes | Serves: 4 | Dairy-Free | Calories: 385

Anything with a festive twist is a winner for us! These scotch eggs are great for snacking on, but we also love to have them as part of a ploughman's-style platter.

## INGREDIENTS

6 free-range eggs

750g 5% fat turkey mince

2 tsp dried sage

2 tsp onion granules

1 tsp fine sea salt

3 slices of wholemeal bread

4 tbsp cranberry sauce

## METHOD

Preheat the oven to 200°c/180°c fan.

Put 4 of the eggs into a large saucepan and cover completely with cold water (the water should be about 1 inch above the eggs). Turn to a medium-high heat and, as soon as it starts to boil, set a timer for 3 and a half minutes.

Meanwhile, prepare a bowl of ice-cold water. When the timer goes off, transfer the eggs to the cold water and leave for a minimum of 15 minutes.

Mix the turkey mince, sage, onion granules, salt and one of the remaining eggs together in a bowl.

Carefully peel the boiled eggs while in the water and place them on a clean paper towel. (The eggs will be very soft so try not to break them.)

Toast the bread, allow it to cool, then blend to a crumb and transfer to a bowl or plate. Crack the final egg into a second bowl and whisk.

Split the seasoned turkey mince into 4 equal portions and flatten out to create a patty approximately 1cm thick.

Now for the fiddly bit: hold the patty in your palm and spoon half a tablespoon of cranberry sauce into the centre. Then, pop a boiled egg into the middle. Wetting your hands with clean cold water will help to stop the meat from sticking to your palm.

Cup your hand to bring the meat over the egg and, before closing the gap, spoon another half tablespoon of cranberry sauce on top.

Seal the gap and carefully mould into a tight ball, making sure there are no gaps.

Coat in a very thin layer of beaten egg, then roll in breadcrumbs. Repeat with the remaining boiled eggs and turkey mince.

Place the scotch eggs on a non-stick ovenproof tray, spray with cooking oil spray and cook for 30 minutes.

# GIANT YORKSHIRE PUDDING WRAP

Prep time: 5 minutes | Cooking time: 35 minutes | Serves: 2 | Calories: 600

This recipe is made using all the leftovers from a Sunday roast. We often include chicken, stuffing and vegetables, but you could wrap any leftovers up in this giant, fluffy Yorkshire pudding!

## INGREDIENTS

**For the Yorkshire pudding**

3 medium eggs

150ml semi-skimmed milk

3 tbsp plain flour

Pinch of fine sea salt

Cooking oil spray

**For the filling**

Roast dinner leftovers (we love to use roast chicken, stuffing, potatoes, and carrots)

Gravy

## METHOD

Preheat the oven to 220°c/200°c fan.

To make the giant Yorkshire puddings, whisk the flour, eggs, milk and salt together in a bowl to make a smooth batter.

Spray two 20cm x 20cm cake tins with cooking oil spray and pop into the preheated oven for 10 minutes.

Remove the tins when red-hot and pour half the Yorkshire pudding mixture into each, then return them to the oven (make sure to do this step quickly!).

Cook for 20-25 minutes until the puddings have risen and turned a nice golden colour but be careful not to open the door while they're cooking. While they're in the oven, reheat the fillings ready for assembly.

Remove the Yorkshire puddings from their tins and flatten them using a large clean chopping board, then fill with your desired fillings and a drizzle of gravy.

Carefully fold and wrap in greaseproof paper or kitchen foil.

Place the wraps on an ovenproof tray and pop them back into the oven to crisp up to your liking.

Remove and serve immediately with a pot of hot gravy.

# PIGS IN A HOLE

Prep time: 5 minutes | Cooking time: 25 minutes | Serves: 12 | Calories: 82 each one

We have been making this Yorkshire pudding recipe for years; it's super easy and so versatile. Toad in the hole is an absolute classic and swapping out the plain sausages for pigs in blankets gives it that festive twist!

## INGREDIENTS

3 tbsp plain flour

3 medium eggs

150ml semi-skimmed milk

Pinch of fine sea salt

12 pigs in blankets

Cooking oil spray

## METHOD

Preheat the oven to 230°c/210°c fan.

Whisk the flour, egg, milk and salt together in a bowl to make a smooth batter.

Spray a 12-cup muffin tin with cooking oil, then place a pig in blanket into each cup. Pop the tray into the centre of the oven and heat for 5 minutes until smoking hot.

Remove the tray and quickly pour the batter into each cup so that it covers bottom of the tin, then return to the oven (speed is of the essence here!).

Cook for 20 minutes, or until risen and a nice golden colour. (But don't open the door while they're cooking.)

## NOTES

Serve with roast potatoes, veg and a dollop of cranberry sauce.

# STICKY CRANBERRY CHICKEN

Prep time: 15 minutes | Cooking time: 20 minutes | Serves: 2 | Calories: 340

Cranberry sauce goes with everything during the festive period, but why not try it at any time of year? This recipe uses it in a slightly different way to make a beautiful sticky sauce.

## INGREDIENTS

2 chicken breasts

1 egg

25g cornflour

Cooking oil spray

4 tbsp cranberry sauce

3 tbsp water

1 tbsp honey

## METHOD

Preheat the oven to 190°c/170°c fan and cut the chicken breasts into goujons or strips.

In a large shallow bowl, whisk the egg and then add the chicken. Turn until well coated.

Place the cornflour in a separate bowl. Piece by piece, add the chicken to the cornflour, turning until each piece is fully coated.

Place the coated chicken pieces on a non-stick baking tray and spray them with oil, then cook in the preheated oven for 15-20 minutes until golden and crispy.

Meanwhile, combine the cranberry sauce, water and honey in a saucepan. Heat through until the sauce is bubbling and starts to thicken.

When the chicken is cooked, add it to the sauce and mix through until every piece is covered. Serve immediately.

## NOTES

We like to serve this chicken in pitta or flatbreads, with a side of tasty garlic and sage fries.

The chicken can be cooked in the oven as above, or in an air fryer at 200°c for 15 minutes.

# STICKY CHICKS
# IN BLANKETS

Prep time: 10 minutes | Cooking time: 10 minutes | Serves: 16 | Calories: 41 each one

We absolutely love this simple, sticky sauce, but we've given it a bit of a festive twist and swapped out the traditional pigs for chicks! These are perfect for buffets and sharing platters but can also be enjoyed as a side to a main dish or even as a snack.

## INGREDIENTS

8 chicken sausages

8 rashers of streaky bacon

3 tbsp balsamic vinegar

2 tbsp runny honey

2 tbsp soy sauce

½ tsp cinnamon

½ tsp nutmeg

## METHOD

Cut each sausage and piece of streaky bacon in half, then wrap each piece of bacon around a sausage and place into the air fryer pan (with the ends of the bacon facing down).

Cook for about 10 minutes at 190°c.

Meanwhile, make the sticky sauce by adding the remaining ingredients to a pan on a medium heat. Cook for around 2-3 minutes or until it bubbles and starts to thicken.

Turn the heat off and add the chicks in blankets to the pan, stirring carefully so that they become covered in the sticky sauce.

Serve immediately and enjoy.

### NOTES

This recipe can be scaled up or down depending on the amount of streaky bacon and sausages you have.

# FESTIVE PASTA BAKE

Prep time: 15 minutes | Cooking time: 40 minutes | Serves: 4-6 | Calories: 530

Our festive pasta bake always makes an appearance in December! It contains loads of traditional Christmas food and flavours but they're all incorporated into a delicious cheesy tomato pasta! It's great for using up Christmas leftovers (if there ever are any!).

## INGREDIENTS

Cooking oil spray

1 onion, chopped

2 chicken breasts, diced

400g passata

1 x 400g tin of chopped tomatoes

3 tbsp tomato relish (optional)

2 tsp sage

1 tsp rosemary

1 tsp garlic granules

300g dried pasta

80g light cheddar, grated

80g mozzarella, grated

100g stuffing

4 tbsp cranberry sauce

8 pigs in blankets, part cooked (we use our Sticky Chicks in Blankets, see page 152)

## METHOD

Preheat the oven to 210°c/190°c fan.

Add cooking oil spray to a large pan and fry the onion until softened. Then, add the chicken and fry for a further 5 minutes.

Add the passata, tinned tomatoes, relish, sage, rosemary and garlic. Stir through and simmer for 10-15 minutes.

Meanwhile, in a separate pan, cook the pasta until al dente.

Drain the pasta and stir it through the sauce, then transfer to an ovenproof dish.

Mix the cheddar and mozzarella together in a bowl, then fold half of the cheese mix into the pasta. Sprinkle the rest over the top of the dish.

Break up the stuffing and arrange it over the top, then add dollops of cranberry sauce and finish with the pigs or chicks in blankets.

Pop in the oven for 20 minutes and leave to cool slightly before serving.

## NOTES

This one will freeze well and it's great for reheating in the oven or microwave.

# CURRYWURST

Prep time: 10 minutes | Cooking time: 30 minutes | Serves: 2 | Gluten-Free, Dairy-Free | Calories: 565

A Christmas market tradition! Bratwursts are one of Clinton's favourites and currywurst is always a must during the festive period. This healthier version means it can be enjoyed at home all year round.

## INGREDIENTS

3-4 medium potatoes

2 bratwurst sausages

1 white onion, diced

1 clove of garlic, crushed

½ tsp cinnamon

1 tsp paprika

2 tbsp medium curry powder

1 x 400g tin of chopped tomatoes

1 tbsp tomato purée

150ml chicken stock

## METHOD

Cut the potatoes into chips and pop them in an air fryer or a preheated oven at 200°c/180°c fan. Cook for 25 minutes.

Cook the bratwurst in a preheated grill for 15 minutes, turning halfway through.

Meanwhile, add some cooking oil spray to a pan and fry the onions and garlic until softened.

Stir in the cinnamon, paprika and curry powder and cook for 2-3 minutes.

Take off the heat and add the chopped tomatoes and tomato purée.

Add to a blender and blitz until smooth.

Return the sauce to the pan, add the chicken stock, then simmer until reduced and thickened.

Serve the chips on a plate, then slice the bratwurst and place on top of the chips. Cover with the curry sauce and sprinkle with curry powder.

## NOTES

Alternative sausages can be used instead of bratwurst, if desired.

# MINCE PIE BAKLAVA

Prep time: 10 minutes | Cooking time: 30 minutes | Makes 12-18 | Calories: 74 | Contains Nuts

Mince pies and baklava in one... absolute heaven! The sweet, sticky honey taste of baklava with the festive flavours of a mince pie in the middle! This recipe can be made into big or small portions, so they're perfect for a dessert or as part of a buffet.

## INGREDIENTS

Butter-flavoured cooking oil spray

9 sheets of filo pastry

200g mincemeat

4 tbsp water

2 tbsp honey

1 lemon, juiced and zested

5 almonds, finely chopped

## METHOD

Preheat the oven to 210°c /190°c fan.

Line a 20cm x 20cm baking tin with greaseproof paper so it rests over the sides of the tin and can be lifted out. Spray all over with the butter-flavoured cooking oil spray.

Lay 3 sheets of filo in the tin, spraying with cooking spray between each layer.

Mix the mincemeat and water together in a bowl, then spread half of the mincemeat mix over the filo.

Add a further 3 layers of filo, spraying with oil in between, then add another layer of mincemeat before finishing with the final 3 layers of filo (again, spraying oil in between each layer).

Using a sharp knife, cut the baklava into 12 or 18 portions. These can be in squares, triangles, or diamond shapes.

Place the baklava into the middle of the oven and cook for 30 minutes.

Meanwhile, in a pan on a low heat, gently warm the honey, lemon juice and zest.

Once the baklava is cooked, remove it from the oven and, while still warm, pour the honey and lemon mix over the top and finish with a sprinkle of chopped almonds.

Remove from the tin and take a sharp knife through the original cuts to re-cut the portions.

Serve and enjoy.

## NOTES

These are delicious served warm with a scoop of vanilla ice cream.

# POTATO LATKES

Prep time: 20 minutes | Cooking time: 20 minutes | Serves: 10 | Vegetarian, Dairy-Free | Calories: 84 each one

I remember these from growing up and going to celebrations with my grandad. A latke is like a potato fritter which is traditionally made for the Jewish celebration Hannukah, but they can be enjoyed all year round.

## INGREDIENTS

500g potatoes, peeled

1 white onion

½ tsp salt

3 tbsp plain flour

2 eggs

Pinch of pepper

Cooking oil spray

## METHOD

Grate the potato and onion into a bowl, then add the salt and leave for 10 minutes. This will allow any liquid to be released and help them to crisp up when cooked.

Drain the liquid and place the potato and onion onto a clean tea towel. Wrap up and squeeze tightly to get rid of any remaining liquid.

Place back into a bowl, then add the flour, eggs and pepper and mix well.

Spray a frying pan with cooking oil spray and, using a tablespoon, spoon the potato mixture into the pan in rough circle shapes. You should fit 3-4 in the pan at a time.

Fry on one side for 3-4 minutes then carefully flip over and repeat on the other side until the latkes are golden and crispy.

Once cooked, place onto a plate and repeat the process with the remaining mixture.

Optional: Heat the latkes through in the air fryer once cooked before serving.

## NOTES

Serve with apple sauce or our Sour Cream dip (see page 136).

# STICKY KOREAN CHICKEN DRUMSTICKS

Prep time: 10 minutes, plus 30 minutes marinating | Cooking time: 30 minutes | Serves: 12 | Calories: 210

Chicken drumsticks always make us think of summer and barbecues in the garden, but these can be enjoyed all year round and cooked in the oven or air fryer. They make a lovely alternative to chicken breast as a main meal, but they're great for parties, picnics, and buffets too.

## INGREDIENTS

12 chicken drumsticks

2 tbsp honey

2 tbsp gochujang paste

2 tbsp soy sauce

2 tbsp tomato purée

2 cloves of garlic, crushed and chopped

1 tsp sesame oil

Cooking oil spray

Sesame seeds, to serve

Spring onion, chopped, to serve

## METHOD

Mix the honey, gochujang, soy sauce, tomato purée, garlic and sesame oil in a large bowl until well combined.

Add the chicken drumsticks and stir to coat. Pop in the fridge and leave to marinate for 30 minutes or overnight.

Preheat the oven to 210°c/190°c fan.

Line a baking tray with greaseproof paper, then place the drumsticks onto the tray and pour over any marinade that might be left in the bowl. Spray with cooking oil spray and cook for 15 minutes.

Turn the drumsticks over and spoon any sauce from the tray over the top. Spray again with cooking oil spray and cook for a further 15 minutes.

Once cooked, sprinkle with sesame seeds and chopped spring onion to serve.

## NOTES

Try these on the barbecue for a beautiful, charred flavour or in the air fryer for quicker cooking.

# SPOOKY PUMPKIN SOUP

Prep time: 5 minutes | Cooking time: 30 minutes | Serves: 4 | Vegetarian, Gluten-Free*, Dairy-Free | Calories: 39

If you've been carving pumpkins for Halloween and have all the flesh left over, then this soup is perfect. With just a hint of spice, this one's a lovely autumnal warmer.

## INGREDIENTS

1 white onion, chopped

1 clove of garlic, chopped

Cooking oil spray

600g pumpkin flesh, roughly diced

1 tsp chilli powder

1 tsp ginger

1 tsp smoked paprika

600ml vegetable stock*

Roasted pumpkin seeds (optional, to serve)

## METHOD

Spray a saucepan with cooking oil and fry the onion and garlic for 3-4 minutes on a medium heat until slightly browned. Then, add the pumpkin, chilli powder, ginger and smoked paprika and fry for a further 2-3 minutes.

Pour in the vegetable stock and use a wooden spoon to scrape all the flavour from the bottom of the pan.

Bring to the boil, then turn down to a simmer for 20 minutes.

Blend with a hand blender until smooth and serve with roasted pumpkin seeds on top.

## NOTES

This will keep in the fridge for up to a week, so it's perfect for lunches at work.

# BONFIRE CHILLI

Prep time: 15 minutes | Cooking time: 45 minutes | Serves: 4-6 | Gluten-Free, Dairy-Free | Calories: 230

Imagine standing round a bonfire with hot chilli and a jacket potato. This warming dish is great for making in a large batch when hosting a bonfire party, but it can also be enjoyed any time of the year.

## INGREDIENTS

Cooking oil spray

1 large onion, diced

2 cloves of garlic, crushed

1 red bell pepper, chopped

500g 5% fat beef steak mince

6 closed cup mushrooms, sliced

1 red chilli, chopped, or 1 tsp dried chilli flakes

2 tbsp tomato purée

1 x 400g tin of chopped tomatoes

1 tsp paprika

1 tsp ground cumin

1 tsp chilli powder

1 tsp ground coriander

½ tsp ground cinnamon

2 bay leaves

1 x 400g tin of kidney beans, drained

1 beef stock cube

2 tbsp Worcestershire sauce or Henderson's Relish

## METHOD

Spray a large pan with cooking oil spray and fry the onions and garlic for 5 minutes on a medium heat. Add the peppers and cook for a further 5 minutes.

Add the beef steak mince and cook until browned, then add the mushrooms and chilli and cook for a further 2-3 minutes.

Add the tomato purée, stir through, then add all the remaining ingredients.

Stir, cover, and simmer for 30 minutes.

# ON THE SIDE

# SPETSOFAI

Prep time: 10 minutes | Cooking time: 45 minutes | Serves: 2 | Calories: 234

This is one of Zoe's favourite traditional Greek dishes. It's a rich sausage and tomato casserole-style dish and it's perfect as a main meal, a smaller serving for a starter, or as part of a meze.

## INGREDIENTS

Cooking oil spray

130g reduced fat smoked sausage, sliced 0.5cm thick

1 onion, sliced

1 red pepper, sliced

1 yellow pepper, sliced

2 cloves of garlic, chopped

2 tbsp red wine vinegar

1 tbsp tomato purée

1 x 400g tin of chopped tomatoes

2 tsp smoked paprika

1 tsp oregano

2 bay leaves

100ml water

## METHOD

Heat some cooking oil spray in a deep frying pan, then add the sliced sausage and cook for 2-3 minutes on a low heat.

Add the onion and pepper and cook for 5 minutes, then add the chopped garlic and cook for a further 5 minutes.

Turn the heat up to medium and add the red wine vinegar. Stir through then add the tomato purée and cook for 2-3 minutes.

Add the tinned tomatoes, smoked paprika, oregano, and bay leaves. Stir through, then add the water and season to taste with salt and pepper. Pop the lid on and simmer for 15 minutes.

Remove the lid, stir, and cook for another 15 minutes until reduced and thickened.

## NOTES

This recipe can also be cooked in a slow cooker just like a sausage casserole. Fry off the sausage, onion, pepper, and garlic, then pop into a slow cooker with the remaining ingredients at medium for about 2-3 hours.

# EASY FLATBREADS

Prep time: 5 minutes | Cooking time: 5 minutes | Serves: 2 | Calories: 155

This dough recipe is like magic: it's only 2 ingredients and it's made in a matter of minutes! We've been making these for years now and have adapted it to make many other dishes, like pizzas, calzones, tacos and naan.

## INGREDIENTS

75g self-raising flour
80g authentic Greek yoghurt

## METHOD

Mix the flour and yoghurt together in a bowl to form a dough. Then, split the dough into 2 pieces and roll into balls.

Roll each ball out into a flatbread shape, about 2mm thick.

Place each flatbread into a non-stick frying pan and dry fry on a medium-high heat for 2 minutes. Then, flip over and cook the other side. When it has puffed up a little, it's cooked and ready to enjoy.

## NOTES

Try to use authentic Greek yoghurt as it's thicker; this way, you won't need any additional flour for rolling.

Try adding crushed garlic and chopped fresh coriander to the dough to make a naan-style flatbread.

# HONEY BAKED FILO FETA

Prep time: 5 minutes | Cooking time: 20 minutes | Serves: 2 | Vegetarian | Calories: 324

One of our favourite restaurants in Corfu makes the best version of this: soft, hot cheese and crispy, sweet filo is a beautiful combination. We created this recipe so that we could enjoy it at home too!

## INGREDIENTS

2 sheets of filo pastry

Cooking oil spray

180g Greek feta

2 tbsp honey

1 tsp sesame seeds

## METHOD

Preheat the oven to 190°c/170°c fan. Lay 1 sheet of filo pastry on your work surface, then spray the pastry with oil. Place the second sheet over the top and spray again.

Place the block of feta in the middle of the pastry on its narrowest edge. Begin to roll the filo over the feta. Fold the edges of the filo in and roll the feta to the end of the sheet, ensuring the whole block is covered.

Place the filo parcel into a small baking dish with the folds underneath to keep it closed. Spray with cooking spray oil, then bake for approximately 15 minutes.

Drizzle the parcel with 1 tablespoon of the honey, then place back into the oven for a further 2-3 minutes.

Remove from the oven, drizzle with the other tablespoon of honey and top with sesame seeds to finish.

# GRILLED MIXED MUSHROOMS

Prep time: 10 minutes | Cooking time: 10 minutes | Serves: 1 | Vegetarian, Gluten-Free | Calories: 80

Clinton immediately fell in love with this starter after trying it at one of our favourite restaurants in Corfu. Our healthier version still has all the wonderful nutty flavours of the mushrooms and is super easy to make.

## INGREDIENTS

150g oyster mushrooms

2 portobello mushrooms

1 tsp fresh cut thyme

1 tsp fresh cut rosemary

1 clove of garlic, crushed and chopped

1 tbsp Henderson's Relish

Cooking oil spray

1 tsp fine sea salt

45g ricotta

## METHOD

Clean and prep the mushrooms (do not wash the mushrooms, just wipe them with a damp, clean cloth.)

Slice the portobello mushrooms and combine them with the oyster mushrooms, herbs, garlic and Henderson's Relish in a large bowl.

Heat a large frying pan or skillet over a medium-high heat and spray with cooking oil spray. Then, add the mushrooms to the pan and cook for 3-4 minutes, making sure not to crowd them.

After 3-4 minutes, carefully turn the mushrooms over and cook for a further 3-4 minutes until tender and golden-brown.

Serve with a sprinkling of salt and a dollop of ricotta on top.

# KACHUMBER SALAD

Prep time: 15 minutes | Serves: 2 | Vegetarian, Dairy-Free, Gluten-Free | Calories: 24

Kachumber is a super simple chopped salad. It often accompanies Indian dishes, which is when we usually enjoy it, but it's also great as a summer salad at barbecues or for eating as a dip with pitta breads or poppadoms.

## INGREDIENTS

1 large tomato, diced

1 red onion, diced

10cm length of cucumber, diced

2 tbsp fresh coriander, chopped

1 tbsp fresh mint, chopped

1 green chilli, finely chopped

½ lemon, juiced and zested

1 tsp fine sea salt

½ tsp cumin

## METHOD

Add the diced tomato, red onion, and cucumber to a bowl with a pinch of salt. Stir and leave to stand for 10 minutes.

Drain any liquid from the bowl then stir in the chopped herbs, chilli, lemon juice, salt, and cumin.

Mix until combined, then top with the lemon zest and serve.

# TURKISH BULGUR PILAF

Prep time: 15 minutes | Cooking time: 25 minutes | Serves: 3 | Calories: 275

A popular side with many Turkish dishes, we often have this with flatbreads or grilled kebabs. It also makes a great dinner, as it can be eaten hot or cold.

## INGREDIENTS

Cooking oil spray

1 sweet red or orange pepper, finely chopped

1 small white onion, finely chopped

2 tomatoes, chopped

2 tbsp tomato purée

200g coarse bulgur wheat

350ml vegetable stock

Pinch of salt and pepper

## METHOD

Spray a pan with oil, then fry the chopped pepper and onion until they begin to soften.

Stir in the tomato and cook for 2-3 minutes, then add the tomato purée and bulgur wheat.

Mix well, then pour in the vegetable stock and add the salt and pepper.

Bring to the boil, then turn the heat down low and cover the pan with a lid.

Simmer for 10 minutes or until all the liquid has been absorbed.

Remove from the heat, leave to stand for 2 minutes, then fluff with a fork before serving.

# SAAG RICE

Prep time: 10 minutes | Cooking time: 30 minutes | Serves: 2 | Vegetarian, Dairy-Free, Gluten-Free | Calories: 225

Saag is often translated into English as 'leafy greens.' After trying this spinach-based rice dish at a local Indian restaurant, it became a firm favourite of ours, and we just had to recreate it so we could enjoy it at home.

## INGREDIENTS

100g basmati rice

200ml water

Cooking oil spray

150g baby spinach (washed)

1 white onion, chopped

2 cloves of garlic, chopped

½ tsp coriander seeds

3 whole cloves

½ tsp fine sea salt

½ tsp ground ginger

½ tsp garam masala

## METHOD

Rinse the rice and add to a pan. Add 200ml of cold water, cover with a lid and bring to a boil. Turn down to a simmer and cook for 20 minutes. Remove from the heat and keep covered for 10 minutes.

Meanwhile, heat some cooking oil spray in a large pan, add the spinach, and cook for 1 minute until wilted. Remove and set aside.

Add the onion and garlic to the frying pan and cook for 5 minutes until they start to soften. Stir in the coriander seeds, whole cloves, salt, ginger and garam masala and cook for a further 2-3 minutes.

Add the wilted spinach to the pan and stir through, removing the whole cloves as you find them.

Add the cooked rice and stir gently for 30 seconds before serving.

## NOTES

This recipe is the perfect accompaniment to a homemade Indian curry, like our Butter Chicken (see page 58).

# OUR FANTASTIC FRIES

Prep time: 5 minutes | Cooking time: 25 minutes | Serves: 2 | Vegetarian, Dairy-Free, Gluten-Free | Calories: 300

Fries or chips are our number one on the potato hierarchy and feature in at least 3 of our meals a week. We've had our paddle-style air fryer for a very long time, so we've always been able to enjoy chips in a healthier way. We cut our fries using a chipping gadget, but the recipe below explains how to do it without.

## INGREDIENTS

4 medium potatoes

Cooking oil spray

Chip spice

## METHOD

Cut the potatoes into 1cm thick slices, then lay flat and cut into chips approximately 1cm thick.

Place these into the paddle air fryer and coat liberally with cooking oil spray and a sprinkling of chip spice.

Cook for 15 minutes at 150°c, open the lid and spray with more cooking oil spray, then cook for a further 12 minutes at 180°c.

Sprinkle with more chip spice and serve.

## NOTES

This method is for the paddle-style air fryer; if using a drawer-style one, then you will need to shake the chips part way through cooking. If using a traditional oven, cook at 180°c/160°c fan for 15 minutes then turn up to 210°c/190°c and cook for a further 15 minutes, shaking part way through.

# BOMBAY POTATOES

Prep time: 10 minutes | Cooking time: 10 minutes | Serves: 3-4 | Vegetarian, Dairy-Free, Gluten-Free | Calories: 149

Delicious Indian spiced roast potatoes! These are one of the most popular sides in Indian restaurants, but this recipe means you can enjoy them at home too!

## INGREDIENTS

4-5 medium potatoes, peeled and diced

2 tsp turmeric

Cooking oil spray

1 clove of garlic, crushed and chopped

1 small red onion, chopped

1 tsp paprika

½ tsp cumin

½ tsp mild chilli powder

Pinch of salt and pepper

Fresh coriander leaves, to serve

## METHOD

Preheat the oven to 210°c/190°c fan.

Place the potatoes into a pan of water and add 1 teaspoon of turmeric. Bring to the boil then cook for 5 minutes or until slightly softened.

Meanwhile, spray a large frying pan with cooking oil spray and fry the garlic and red onion for 5 minutes.

Drain the potatoes and transfer to a large bowl. Add the fried onion and garlic and the remaining dried spices and give it a good mix to coat the potatoes.

Transfer to a baking dish or tray, spray with cooking oil spray and bake in the oven for 15 minutes.

Serve with a sprinkle of fresh coriander.

# CRUNCHY ASIAN SLAW

Prep time: 15 minutes | Serves: 2 | Vegetarian, Dairy-Free, Gluten-Free | Calories: 62

A lovely, easy side dish that's super fresh and packed with flavour. It's like a traditional coleslaw with the shredded cabbage, but with the punchiness and tang of South Asian food and flavours.

## INGREDIENTS

1 carrot, grated

¼ red or white cabbage, shredded

½ red pepper, thinly sliced

2 spring onions, thinly sliced

1 clove of garlic, finely grated

20g fresh ginger, grated or ½ tsp of ginger paste

1 tsp sesame seeds

1 tsp honey

½ lime, juiced and zested

## METHOD

Add all the ingredients to a large bowl and stir well to combine.

## NOTES

We love to serve this slaw with chicken satay skewers or Thai-style fish cakes. Try it paired with our Sweet Chilli Salmon and Halloumi Skewers (see page 86).

# ACKNOWLEDGEMENTS AND THANK YOUS

We wouldn't be where we are today, nor have had the opportunity to write this book, without you guys and our amazing Instagram community. The encouragement and support we get from you day in, day out is incredible, and your recipe recreations and lovely comments mean the absolute world to us. You have helped change our lives in more ways than you can imagine, and we truly thank you for this!

A huge thank you to our family and close friends who are always our biggest cheerleaders! When it's been tough or when neither of us have believed in ourselves, you've been there to give us the confidence we needed. You are our greatest motivation, and we love you!

To our main man Taiyo, our world! You are always there by our feet, giving us the motivation to do what we do. (Even if you're more likely only there to see if we drop anything on the floor.)

And finally, to our amazing publisher. If you'd never reached out to us that day, our dreams would never have become a reality. Thank you for all the help, support and patience you have given us to be able to put all this together. The quote on my work desktop calendar that very day read:

"If you have a dream, a vision, an urge for something greater – something that keeps calling you – please don't ignore it. Trust yourself to be able to make it your reality. Look for the signs, believe in yourself, and build up that positive energy."

Thank you from the bottom of our hearts!

Zoe & Clinton

# The Navarros' Kitchen

©2023 Zoe & Clinton Navarro &
Meze Publishing Limited

First edition printed in 2023 in the UK

ISBN: 978-1915538185

Written by: Zoe & Clinton Navarro

Edited by: Emily Readman

Photography by: Carl Sukonik & Timm Cleasby

Designed by: Paul Cocker & Phil Turner

PR: Emma Toogood & Lizzy Capps

Contributors: Katie Fisher

Printed and bound in the UK by
Bell & Bain Ltd, Glasgow

Published by Meze Publishing Limited
Unit 1b, 2 Kelham Square
Kelham Riverside
Sheffield S3 8SD
Web: www.mezepublishing.co.uk
Telephone: 0114 275 7709
Email: info@mezepublishing.co.uk